Prepared in cooperation with the County of Hawai'i Department of Public Works

Potential Effects of Roadside Dry Wells on Groundwater Quality on the Island of Hawai'i— Assessment Using Numerical Groundwater Models

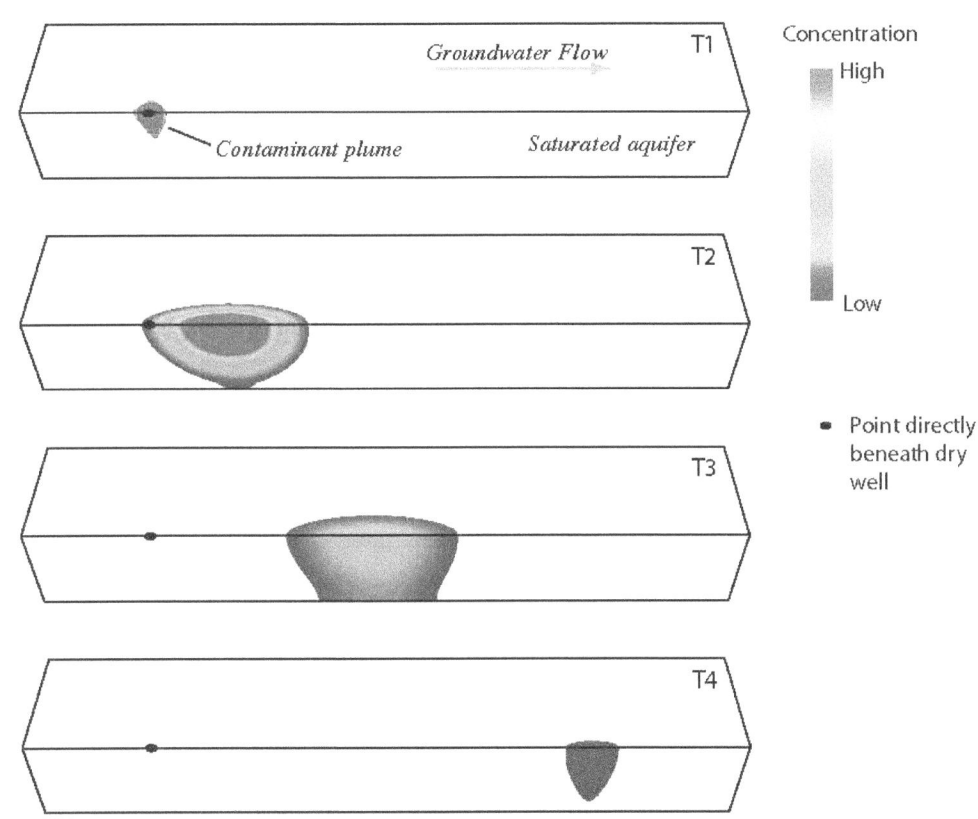

Scientific Investigations Report 2011–5072

U.S. Department of the Interior
U.S. Geological Survey

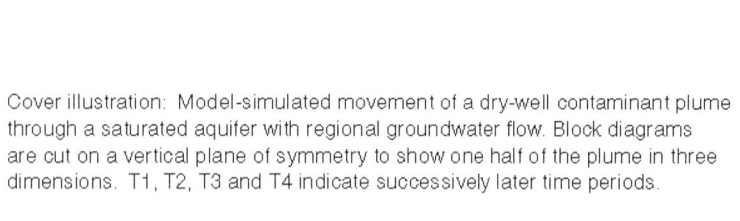

Cover illustration: Model-simulated movement of a dry-well contaminant plume
through a saturated aquifer with regional groundwater flow. Block diagrams
are cut on a vertical plane of symmetry to show one half of the plume in three
dimensions. T1, T2, T3 and T4 indicate successively later time periods.

Potential Effects of Roadside Dry Wells on Groundwater Quality on the Island of Hawai'i— Assessment Using Numerical Groundwater Models

By Scot K. Izuka

Prepared in cooperation with the County of Hawai'i Department of Public Works

Scientific Investigations Report 2011–5072

U.S. Department of the Interior
U.S. Geological Survey

U.S. Department of the Interior
KEN SALAZAR, Secretary

U.S. Geological Survey
Marcia K. McNutt, Director

U.S. Geological Survey, Reston, Virginia: 2011

This report and any updates to it are available online at:
http://pubs.usgs.gov/sir/2011/5072/

For more information on the USGS—the Federal source for science about the Earth, its natural and living resources, natural hazards, and the environment, visit http://www.usgs.gov or call 1-888-ASK-USGS

For an overview of USGS information products, including maps, imagery, and publications, visit http://www.usgs.gov/pubprod

Contents

Figures

Tables

Conversion Factors and Datums

Multiply	By	To obtain
inch (in.)	2.54	centimeter (cm)
foot (ft)	0.3048	meter (m)
mile (mi)	1.609	kilometer (km)
acre	4,047	square meter (m^2)
square foot (ft^2)	0.09290	square meter (m^2)
square mile (mi^2)	2.590	square kilometer (km^2)
foot per mile (ft/mi)	0.1894	meter per kilometer (m/km)
cubic foot (ft^3)	0.02832	cubic meter (m^3)
cubic foot per second (ft^3/s)	0.02832	cubic meter per second (m^3/s)
inch per year (in/yr)	25.4	millimeter per year (mm/yr)
foot per day (ft/d)	0.3048	meter per day (m/d)

Temperature in degrees Celsius (°C) may be converted to degrees Fahrenheit (°F) as follows:

°F=(1.8×°C)+32

Temperature in degrees Fahrenheit (°F) may be converted to degrees Celsius (°C) as follows:

°C=(°F−32)/1.8

Horizontal coordinate information is referenced to the World Geodetic System of 1984 (WGS84).

Elevation refers to distance above mean sea level.

Concentrations of chemical constituents in water are given either in milligrams per liter (mg/L) or micrograms per liter (µg/L).

This page left intentionally blank

Potential Effects of Roadside Dry Wells on Groundwater Quality on the Island of Hawai'i— Assessment Using Numerical Groundwater Models

By Scot K. Izuka

Abstract

Widespread use of dry wells to dispose of roadside runoff has raised concern about the potential effects on the quality of groundwater on the Island of Hawai'i. This study used semi-generic numerical models of groundwater flow and contaminant transport to assess the potential effect of dry wells on groundwater quality on the Island of Hawai'i. The semi-generic models are generalized numerical groundwater-flow and solute-transport models that have a range of aquifer properties and regional groundwater gradients that are characteristic for the island. Several semi-generic models were created to study the effect of dry wells in different hydrogeologic conditions, such as different unsaturated-zone thicknesses or different aquifer characteristics.

Results indicate that mixing of contaminated water from the surface with contaminant-free water in the saturated aquifer immediately reduces the contaminant concentration. The amount the concentration is reduced depends on the hydraulic properties of the aquifer in a given area, the thickness of the unsaturated zone, and whether the infiltration is focused in a small area of a dry well or spread naturally over a larger area.

Model simulations indicate that focusing infiltration of contaminated runoff through a dry well can substantially increase contaminant concentrations in the underlying saturated aquifer relative to infiltration under natural conditions. Simulated concentrations directly beneath a dry well were nearly 8 times higher than the simulated concentrations directly beneath a broad infiltration area representing the natural condition. Where dry wells are present, contaminant concentrations in the underlying saturated aquifer are lower when the unsaturated zone is thicker and higher when the unsaturated zone is thinner. Contaminant concentrations decline quickly as the contaminant plume migrates, with the regional groundwater flow, away from the dry well. The differences among concentrations resulting from the various unsaturated-zone thicknesses also diminish with distance from the dry well. At a horizontal distance of about 700 ft downgradient from the dry well, all simulated maximum concentrations were less than 1 percent of the concentration in the infiltration water; at about 0.5 mi downgradient from the dry well, all simulated concentrations were equal to or less than 0.1 percent. Actual concentrations may be even lower than indicated by the models because of processes such as decay and reaction that were not simulated. Hydrologic and geologic differences from one location to the next also affect contaminant concentrations—simulations using models with properties representative of aquifers in the Hilo area resulted in lower overall concentrations than models with properties representative of aquifers in the Kona area.

Results from this study can be used to assess how contaminants entering a dry well may affect receiving waters in a variety of situations on the Island of Hawai'i. Better assessment would be obtained by using results from models having the most similar conditions (such as climate, hydraulic properties, regional groundwater gradient) to the dry well in question. The results of this study can help determine which dry wells are likely to have the greatest effect on nearby receiving waters and where more specific data and analyses may be needed.

Introduction

More than 2,000 dry wells are used to dispose storm runoff from roads in urbanized areas on the Island of Hawai'i. Most dry wells are in the urbanized areas in the South Hilo District on the east coast and the North Kona District on the west coast (fig. 1). Runoff entering the dry wells may contain contaminants related to automobile traffic, pavement degradation, and deposition of airborne particulates, as well as contaminants that can originate from other activities or incidents that take place in the surface drainage area of the dry well. These contaminants may include metals, oil and grease, fuel and fuel residues, pesticides and other organic compounds, nutrients, and microorganisms (U.S. Environmental Protection Agency, 1994, 1999; De Carlo and Anthony, 2002; Grant and

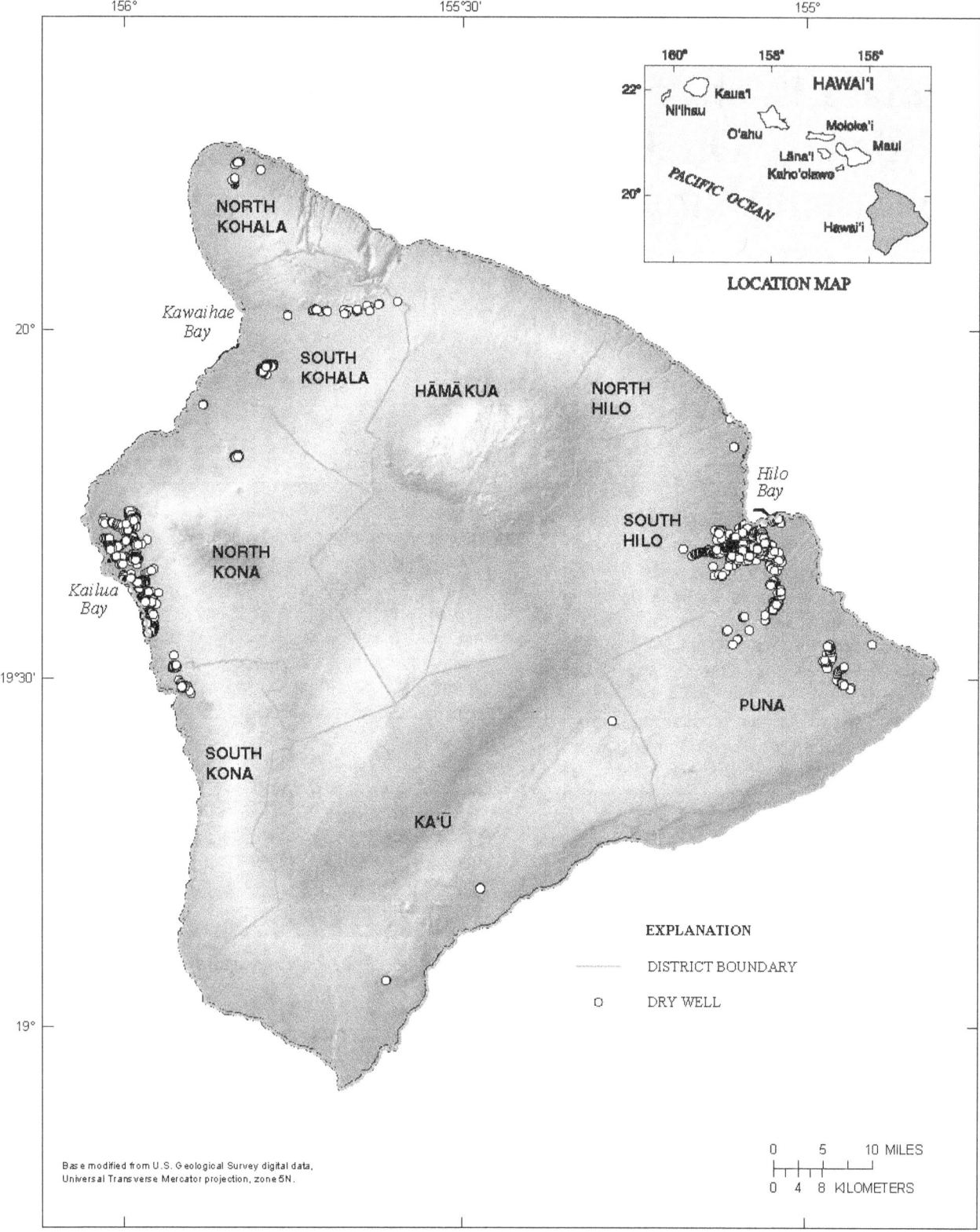

Figure 1.   County of Hawai'i Department of Public Works dry wells. (District boundaries from Hawai'i State Department of Business, Economic Development and Tourism, 2008.)

others, 2003; De Carlo and others 2004; Göbel and others, 2007; Presley and others, 2008). Dry wells are also susceptible to accidental or illicit discharges of hazardous substances (U.S. Environmental Protection Agency, 1999).

Part of the water that flows into and infiltrates the ground through some roadside dry wells comes from runoff that, under natural conditions, would have flowed, along with any water-borne contaminants, to the ocean as surface runoff. Dry wells reroute this water into the groundwater system. Most of the water still ultimately reaches the ocean, but travel time is increased because of the flow resistance provided by the aquifer. Also, in most cases the water discharges at a different location in the ocean than it would have if it remained in the surface-water system. Water-borne contaminants entering dry wells are subject to processes in the groundwater system such as decay or reaction with rock and soil minerals and dilution by mixing with the ambient groundwater. In general, the farther the contaminant travels in the aquifer, the more its concentration will be reduced by these processes. Another part of the water and contaminants that flow into roadside dry wells comes from water that would otherwise have infiltrated the ground over a broad area; dry wells focus the infiltration in a small area. Most dry wells on the Island of Hawai'i penetrate through surface soil and into the underlying rock, thus allowing water to bypass the natural filtering properties of surface soil and vegetation. Dry wells can shorten the paths through which infiltrating water would percolate before reaching the water table, however, the depth of most dry wells on the Island of Hawai'i is much less than the distance between the bottom of the dry well and the water table.

Because the use of dry wells to dispose of roadside runoff is widespread on the Island of Hawai'i, concern has been raised about how the quality of groundwater may be affected, particularly the quality of receiving waters used for water supply and to support coastal ecological systems that are dependent on groundwater. Some developers of new urban areas have been required to take steps to mitigate these concerns (Hawai'i State Land Use Commission, 2002). Such steps are costly, however, and their benefit is difficult to assess because the effect of dry wells on groundwater quality is not known quantitatively.

In 2008–2011, the U.S. Geological Survey (USGS), in cooperation with the County of Hawaii Department of Public Works (DPW), undertook a two-phase study to advance understanding of the potential effects of roadside dry wells on groundwater quality on the Island of Hawai'i. In phase 1, an inventory of all DPW dry wells on the island was compiled and sorted on the basis of criteria that bear on the potential for a dry well to transport contaminants to receiving waters of concern, such as presence or absence of urbanization in the drainage area, distance between the bottom of the dry well and the water table, and proximity to receiving waters (Izuka and others, 2009). In phase 2, which is the subject of this report, numerical modeling was used to assess (1) how the presence of a dry well alters contaminant transport and attenuation relative to natural conditions and (2) how concentrations change as contaminants are transported through the groundwater system from dry wells to receiving waters.

Acknowledgments

This study was funded by a cooperative agreement between the USGS and the County of Hawai'i DPW, Warren Lee, Director. Galen Kuba and Ben Ishii of the DPW provided assistance throughout the study. Delwyn Oki and Charles Hunt of the USGS provided analyses, and helpful suggestions, particularly for the Kona area. The staff of Kaloko-Honokōhau National Historical Park furnished data from monitoring wells. Ka'eo Duarte (Kamehameha Schools) and Stephen Gingerich (USGS) provided helpful technical reviews of the report.

Setting

Hawai'i is the largest (4,030 mi^2) island in the tropical North Pacific Hawaiian archipelago. The island is formed by five large basaltic shield volcanoes: Kohala, Hualālai, Mauna Kea, Mauna Loa, and Kīlauea (fig. 2). Mauna Loa and Mauna Kea each rise above 13,500 ft elevation. Rainfall distribution on the island is influenced by the prevailing northeasterly trade winds and sea breezes generated by diurnal heating and cooling of the large island mass. Precipitation is induced by the orographic effect when the trade winds and sea breezes rise and cool as they encounter the shield volcanoes. Rainfall on the windward (northeastern) slopes of the island can exceed 260 in/yr, whereas on the leeward western coast precipitation is low because of the rain-shadowing effect of the large mountains. The highest land-surface elevations on the interior of the island—particularly the tops of Mauna Kea and Mauna Loa—are arid because the trade-wind inversion limits orographic rainfall to below about 8,200 ft (Giambelluca and others, 1986).

Stream erosion on the Island of Hawai'i is not as advanced as it is on the older islands in the archipelago, but deep valleys have been eroded into the northeastern slope of Kohala and numerous youthful gulches dissect the wet windward-facing slope of Mauna Kea and the southeast slope of Mauna Loa. Stream erosion is less distinct in the drier areas, such as the leeward west side of the island and the arid peaks of Mauna Loa and Mauna Kea. Stream erosion is also less apparent on Kīlauea and most of Mauna Loa, where erosion competes with the formation of new lava terrain from these active volcanoes.

Hydrogeology

The five large shield volcanoes that form the Island of Hawai'i are basaltic mid-plate, hot-spot volcanoes (Stearns and Macdonald, 1946; Macdonald and others, 1983; Peterson and Moore, 1987; Sherrod and others, 2008). The bulk of the

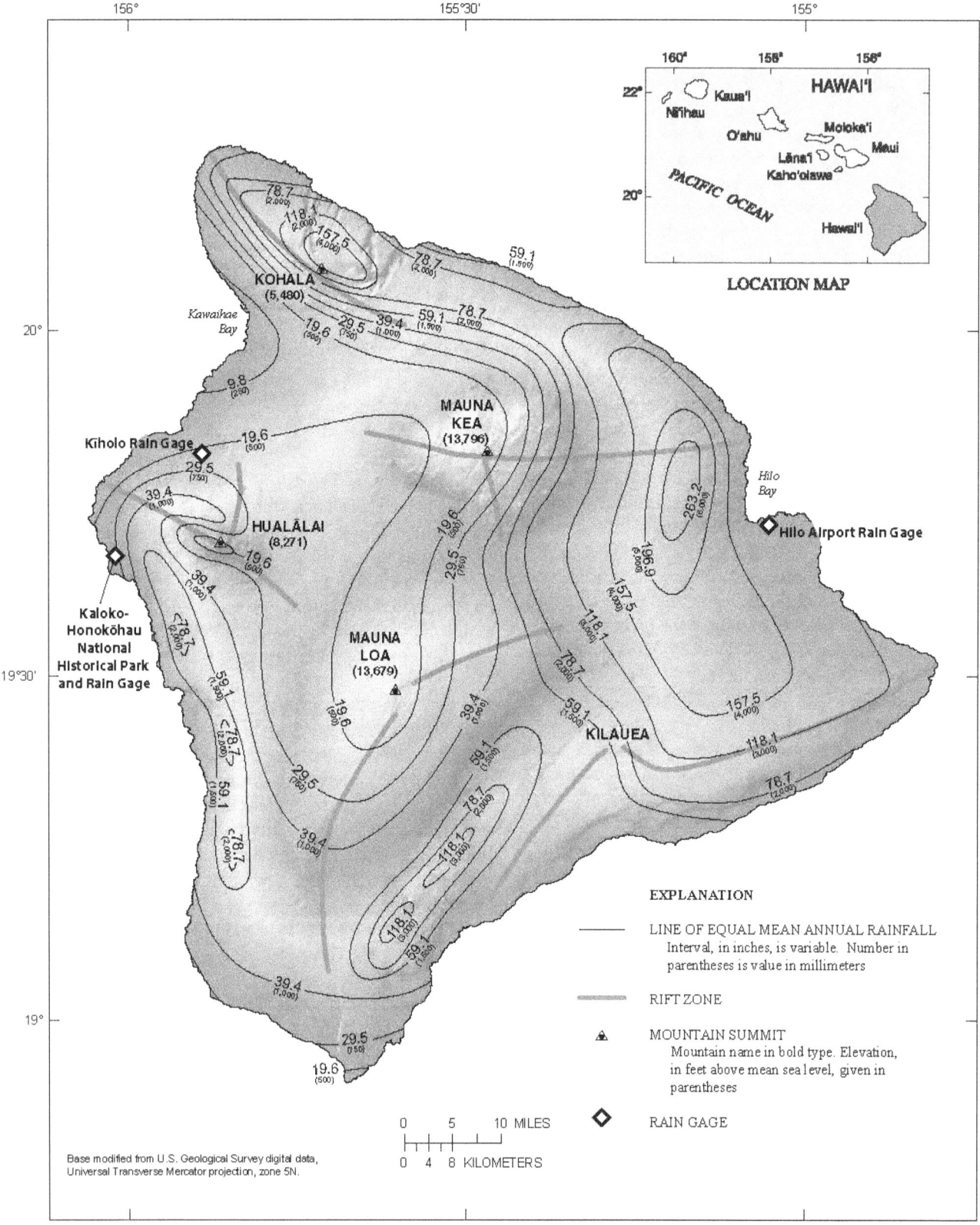

Figure 2.   Major geographic features and rainfall distribution on the Island of Hawai'i. (Rainfall distribution from Giambelluca and others, 1986; rift zones from Peterson and Moore, 1987.)

subaerial portion of these volcanoes is built of thousands of thin tholeiitic-basalt lava flows that originated from eruptions at the summits or along linear rift zones that radiate from the summits (fig. 2). The Island of Hawai'i is geologically the youngest island in the Hawaiian archipelago—radiometric dates indicate that the entire surface of the island is less than 1 million years old (Clague and Dalrymple, 1987). Weathering and soil development are shallower and less extensive on the Island of Hawai'i than on the older islands in the archipelago. Much of the land surface is bare rock, particularly on active parts of volcanoes and where the climate is particularly arid (Sato and others, 1973). The Island of Hawai'i also lacks a substantial sedimentary coastal plain, such as that present on some of the older islands.

The ultimate source of fresh water in oceanic islands is precipitation, which includes rain, snow, and fog. Water from precipitation can run off the land surface to the ocean through streams, infiltrate the subsurface and recharge groundwater, or return to the atmosphere through evapotranspiration (evaporation and transpiration by plants) (fig. 3). Water that infiltrates below the plant root zone passes downward through unsaturated rock until it reaches the saturated part of the aquifer. The top of the saturated aquifer is the water table. Some of the terms used to describe the water passing between the surface and subsurface are used inconsistently in previous literature and can therefore be a source of confusion. In this report, "infiltration" refers to the water entering the subsurface before

it reaches the saturated aquifer; this is referred to as "potential recharge" in some literature. When infiltration reaches the saturated aquifer, it is referred to as "recharge" in this report.

In oceanic islands, fresh water in the saturated part of the aquifer forms a lens-shaped body underlain by salt water from the ocean (fig 3). Between the freshwater lens and the underlying salt water is a zone of mixing containing brackish water. In the natural state, the overall thickness of the freshwater lens depends on the aquifer hydraulic conductivity (a measure of permeability) and rate of groundwater recharge—freshwater lenses are thinner where the hydraulic conductivity is high or groundwater recharge rates are low. The freshwater lens is buoyed by the underlying salt water because fresh water is slightly less dense than salt water. The Ghyben-Herzberg relation, which is based on the buoyancy caused by the density difference, indicates that the thickness of the freshwater lens below sea level is 40 times the elevation of the water table above sea level. The relation assumes hydrostatic conditions that do not exist in the freshwater lens, but yields a reasonable approximation in parts of the freshwater lens where flow is horizontal.

Fresh water in the lens flows naturally from inland areas, where most recharge occurs, to coastal areas, where groundwater discharges to springs, streams, and the ocean. Wells that pump water from the aquifer intercept some of the natural groundwater flow. In some areas, including coastal areas, depressions in the land surface expose the water table (top of the saturated part of the aquifer) (fig. 4). The exposed water

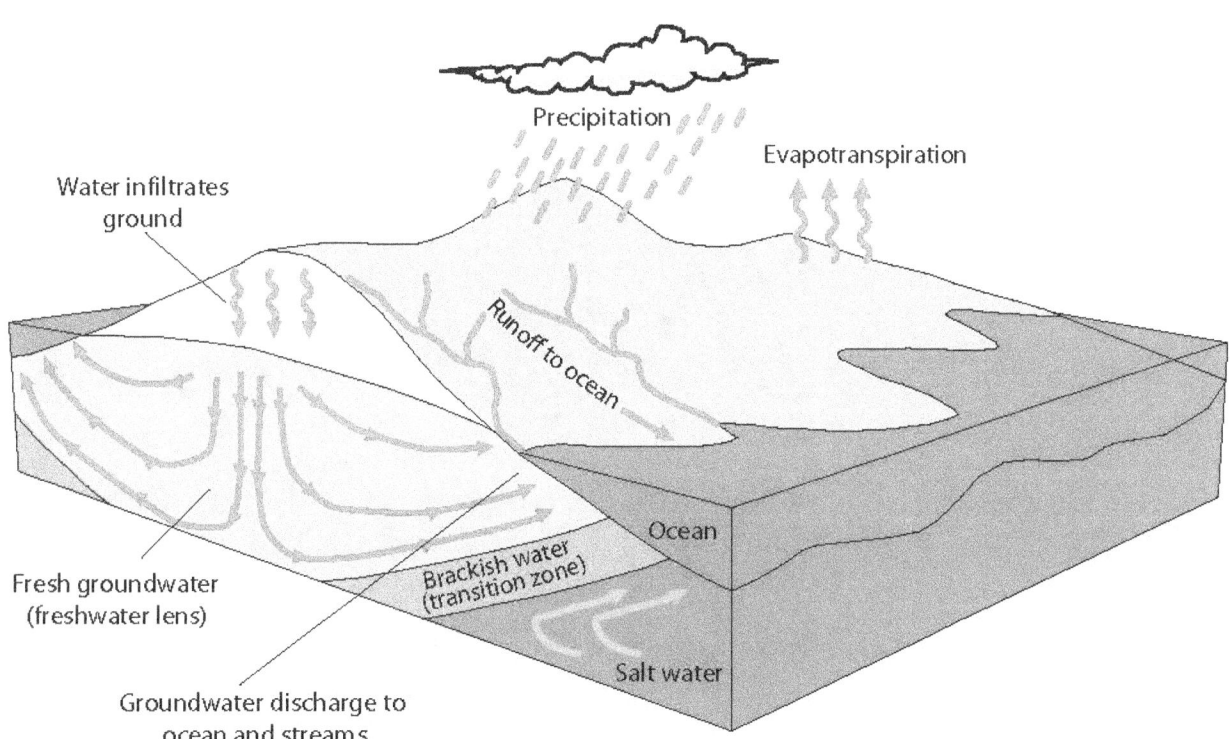

Figure 3. Diagram of hydrologic cycle and groundwater occurrence in tropical islands.

table can take the form of wetlands, lakes, ponds, springs, or persistently flowing streams. These water bodies provide habitats for organisms.

Contaminants reaching the water table beneath inland areas can be transported by regional groundwater flow to receiving waters at the coast. Wells that intercept some of the natural groundwater flow may intercept contaminants carried in the groundwater. Whether the contaminants present a threat to receiving waters or wells depends on the physical, chemical, and biological processes within the aquifer. These processes include dilution, sorption, and degradation, which generally tend to attenuate the contaminants the longer they travel through the aquifer.

The high primary porosity and lack of weathering in the youthful, voluminous lava flows that form the bulk of the Island of Hawai'i result in an aquifer that has relatively high permeability, particularly in the dike-free flanks of the shield volcanoes. Estimates of the hydraulic conductivity for flank lava flows on the Island of Hawai'i are as high as several thousand feet per day (Oki and others, 1999; Oki, 1999, 2002; Whittier and others, 2004). This high-permeability aquifer is volumetrically the primary aquifer on the island. The freshwater lens is thin in most areas as a result of the high permeability. The water table is near sea level at the coast and rises gently a few feet per mile in the inland direction (Stearns and

Macdonald, 1946). The slope of the water table (water-table gradient) and lens thickness can vary, however, as a result of variations in the amount of water flowing through the aquifer or variations in hydraulic conductivity. The slope of the water table is likely to be steeper where the hydraulic conductivity is lower or in wetter climates where recharge is greater. For example, water levels in monitor wells in the Kaloko-Honokōhau National Historical Park on the arid coast of the North Kona District indicate a gradient of about 0.7 ft per mile. In contrast, monitor wells in the South Hilo District on the wetter east coast of the island indicate a gradient of about 5.7 ft per mile.

Few dikes are exposed at the surface on the Island of Hawai'i, but they probably exist beneath the summit and rift zones in all of the island's shield volcanoes (fig. 2). Most dry wells on the Island of Hawai'i are on the flanks of the shield volcanoes (fig. 1), where dikes are probably absent or rare. Some other rocks and structures, such as ash layers, soil and weathered rock, unusually thick lava flows, and lava-draped faults, may also form low-permeability features within the otherwise high-permeability lava-flow pile of the shield volcano (Stearns and Macdonald, 1946; Oki, 1999). Such structures can alter groundwater flow and contaminant transport in some locations. Because the purpose of this study is to assess the effects of dry wells in general on an island-wide basis and not

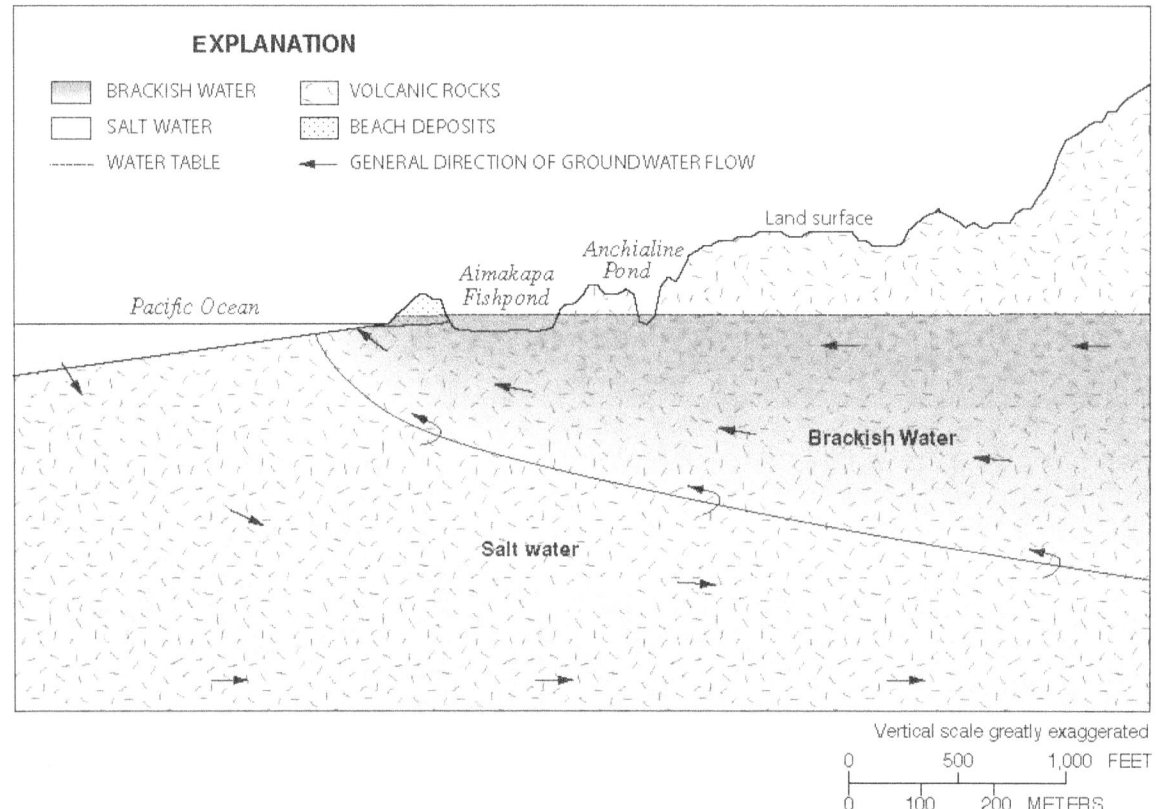

Figure 4. Cross section through the western coast of the Island of Hawai'i showing relation between groundwater and coastal surface-water bodies (from Oki and others, 1999).

to focus on any one locality, simulation of these low-permeability structures was not included in the semi-generic numerical models in this study.

Recent deep exploratory drilling on the Island of Hawai'i indicates that the groundwater hydrology near the juncture of two or more shield volcanoes can be more complex than indicated in the generalized concepts shown in figure 3. A geology-exploration borehole drilled in Hilo indicates the presence of multiple freshwater layers with intervening saltwater layers. The multi-layered freshwater/saltwater system is created by multiple confining units formed at the juncture between Mauna Loa and Mauna Kea (Thomas and others, 1996). Dry wells primarily affect the shallowest of the freshwater layers (the uppermost freshwater lens); the deeper freshwater bodies are recharged at middle elevations on Mauna Kea (Thomas and others, 1996), above most dry wells.

Dry Wells on the Island of Hawai'i

The U.S. Environmental Protection Agency (1999) listed Hawai'i among states that have the highest number of storm-water dry wells in the U.S. Most dry wells in the state are on the Island of Hawai'i. Most DPW dry wells are excavations of about 5 ft in diameter into the porous basalt lava flows of the island (fig. 5). The average DPW dry well is 22 ft deep; 90 percent are between 10 and 30 ft deep (Izuka and others, 2009). The dry wells may be connected to other surface intakes or grouped in roadside swales. As a general rule, dry wells on the Island of Hawai'i are designed to accommodate a flow rate of at least 5 ft³/s (Galen Kuba, DPW, oral commun., 2009).

Dry wells are considered injection wells and are therefore subject to the Federal underground injection control (UIC) programs under the authority of the Safe Drinking Water Act (U.S. Environmental Protection Agency, 1999, 2007). The UIC program primarily protects drinking water, however, and does not specifically address protection of nearshore environments. Dry wells are considered Class V injection wells because they are not expected to dispose of hazardous waste fluids (U.S. Environmental Protection Agency, 2007). Even so, runoff from roadways commonly contains metals and hydrocarbons (U.S. Environmental Protection Agency, 1999; Grant and others, 2003). Dry wells used for storm-water drainage are also susceptible to accidental or illicit deliberate releases of hazardous substances, and contamination related to storm-water runoff has been reported in several states (U.S. Environmental Protection Agency, 1999).

Izuka and others (2009) listed 2,052 dry wells operated by the DPW. Their list included some dry wells with surface drainage areas that encompass high-intensity development, which could be a source of contaminants related to urban land use. Some dry wells in low-lying areas penetrated close to or through the water table, thus eliminating or substantially reducing opportunities for contaminant attenuation between the ground surface and water table. Some dry wells, including some that receive water from areas of high-intensity

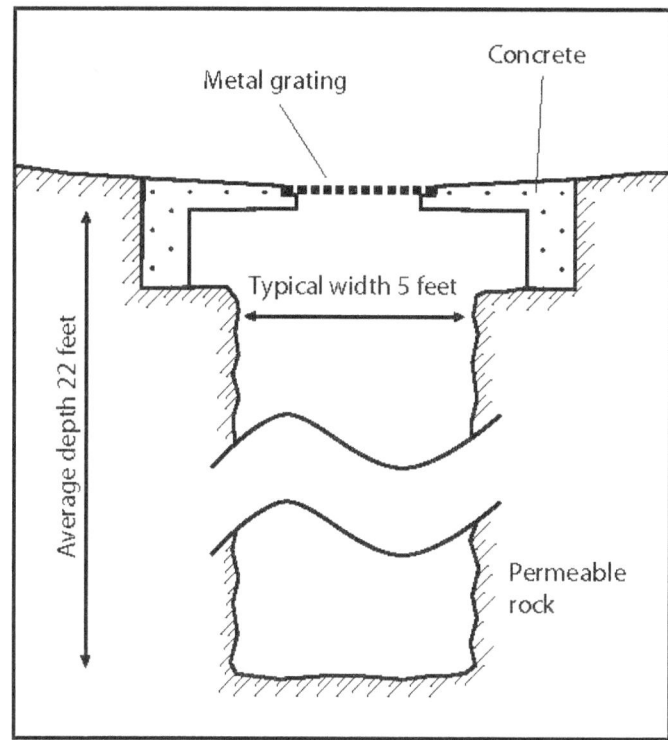

Figure 5.   Sketch of a typical dry well used to dispose of roadside runoff on the Island of Hawai'i (modified from Departments of Public Works of the State of Hawaii, 1984).

development, are close to coastal receiving waters or lie within the areas contributing recharge to drinking-water wells.

Assessment of the Potential Effects of Dry Wells

The objective of this study was to assess the potential effects of dry wells for the entire Island of Hawai'i. However, many factors related to the potential for roadside dry wells to affect groundwater quality (for example groundwater flow paths; the types, initial concentrations, and chemical behavior of contaminants; and the type of receiving waters, their distance from the dry wells, and their sensitivity to contaminant concentration levels) are highly site specific and therefore difficult to study on an island-wide basis. On the other hand, study approaches that do not incorporate at least some representative hydraulic and chemical processes and characteristics may yield results that are too generalized and fail to represent the specific issue for the Island of Hawai'i.

To adequately represent the range of hydrogeologic conditions on the Island of Hawai'i and satisfy the needs for island-wide applicability, this study used semi-generic numerical models of groundwater flow and solute (contaminant) transport. The semi-generic three dimensional rectangular models used in this study do not represent the specific form or geology of any particular location but do represent a range of aquifer properties and conditions that is characteristic for the Island of Hawai'i. In this study, the range is represented by two end-member locations where most of the dry wells on the island are concentrated: (1) the relatively arid coast of the North Kona District and (2) the wetter lowlands of the South Hilo District (figs. 1, 2). Both locations are situated on high-permeability flank lavas of the shield volcanoes but have contrasting climates and groundwater levels. For the purposes of discussion in this report, the region of dry wells in the North Kona District will be referred to as the "Kona area" to distinguish it from the geopolitical North Kona District which encompasses a large and geologically diverse area, not all of which has a significant number of dry wells. For similar purposes and reasons, the region of dry wells in the South Hilo District will be referred to as the "Hilo area" in this report.

The models were further generalized by simulating the transport of only a single, hypothetical, nonreactive contaminant. A nonreactive contaminant does not decay with time or react with the aquifer. The contaminant-attenuation processes simulated by the models are therefore limited to mixing, advection, and dispersion—processes to which all contaminants are subject. Simulating only a single hypothetical nonreactive contaminant eliminates the need to specify what contaminants are likely to be, yet the results can be applied to estimate at least the partial attenuation of any contaminant. Reactive contaminants are likely to be attenuated at least as much as the hypothetical nonreactive contaminant; decay and reaction reduce concentrations of reactive contaminants even further.

The conditions simulated by the semi-generic models in this study likely do not affect, and are unaffected by, the density-dependent freshwater/saltwater relation in the aquifer; therefore it was not necessary to simulate the saltwater part of the aquifer. Also, the hypothetical contaminant was assumed to have the same density as fresh water. Therefore density-dependent flow was not simulated in this study.

The data, time, and resources required to construct a semi-generic model are substantially less than that typically required for a detailed regional model. Because of this simplicity, multiple series of semi-generic models could be created to study contaminant transport over a range of conditions and dry-well/receiving-water relations that are likely to exist on the Island of Hawai'i. The models provide insights on what contaminant concentrations are likely to be at receiving waters, and the results are applicable, with limitations, to most wells on the island.

Conceptual Model of the Relation Between Dry Wells and Groundwater Quality

Development of a conceptual model is the first step in creating any numerical groundwater model. Figure 6 illustrates the conceptual model used in developing the semi-generic

models. In this study, infiltration though a dry well is conceptualized as an event in which the flow rate into the dry well is constant for a finite amount of time—essentially a square pulse. Although the flow rate into a dry well typically varies with time, the simulated square pulse is a simplification that can be replicated easily in the semi-generic models and is a sufficient approximation for the purposes of this study. To facilitate comparisons between different conditions, a pulse of water equivalent to 5 ft^3/s (the design capacity for dry wells on the Island of Hawai'i) flowing for one hour was used for dry-well inflow in all model simulations. Analysis of rainfall data can place this flow rate in perspective with actual storm intensities on the Island of Hawai'i. The highest 1-hour rainfall total recorded during the period of record (2004–2010) for the USGS Kīholo rain gage (fig. 2) in Kona was 2.05 in.; a flow rate of 5 ft^3/s for 1 hour is equivalent to this rainfall rate falling over a drainage area of 1.05×10^5 ft^2 (2.4 acres). In comparison, the climate in Hilo is wetter than in Kona. The highest 1-hour total recorded at the National Weather Service Hilo Airport rain gage was 4.49 in. (National Climatic Data Center, 2010); a flow rate of 5 ft^3/s for 1 hour is equivalent to this rainfall rate falling over an area of only 4.81×10^4 ft^2 (1.1 acres). Rainfall frequency maps (National Weather Service, 2009) indicate that these rainfall rates occur on average about once every 50 to 100 years.

The bottoms of most dry wells are separated by some distance from the water table of the freshwater lens, therefore water from the dry well must infiltrate through an unsaturated zone. The water from the dry well moves downward by gravity through the unsaturated zone until it eventually reaches the water table, where it recharges the freshwater lens and becomes incorporated into the seaward flow of water in the lens. As the pulse of water passes through the unsaturated zone, it becomes drawn out—the thicker the unsaturated zone, the more drawn out the pulse becomes (fig. 6). In this conceptual model, the leading edge of the pulse remains sharp as it moves through the unsaturated zone. Hydraulic properties of the aquifer, particularly vertical hydraulic conductivity (K_v), also affect how the pulse will be drawn out in the unsaturated zone. The unsaturated zone thus affects the rate at which water and contaminants from the dry well recharge the freshwater lens, which in turn affects the concentrations when mixing occurs.

As the pulse of water passes through the unsaturated zone, the concentration of a hypothetical nonreactive contaminant may be affected by evapotranspiration and by mixing with water already present in the unsaturated pores. In the conceptual model for this study, it is assumed that contaminants in the unsaturated zone are transported by advection only, that is, the contaminant travels with the fluid particles (dispersion is assumed to be negligible), and that the concentration of the hypothetical contaminant does not change during its downward migration through the unsaturated zone. The effect of evapotranspiration is likely to be minimal because, in most cases, the water will have been injected far below the reach of physical surface evaporation or the transpiring roots of plants. The effect of mixing with preexisting pore water

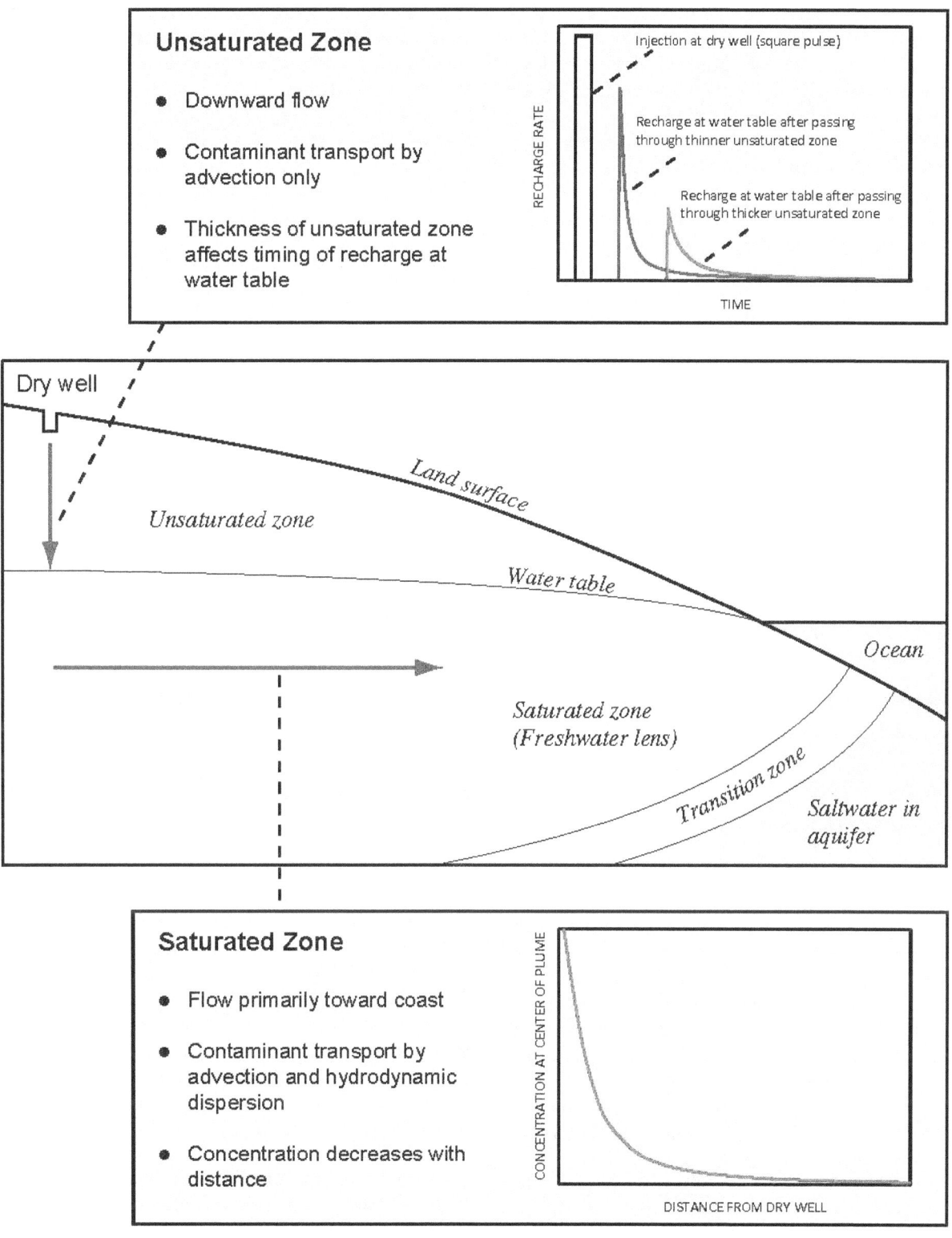

Figure 6. Conceptual model for developing semi-generic numerical groundwater models to study the potential effects of dry wells on groundwater quality on the Island of Hawai'i.

is also assumed to be minimal because the volume of pore water is small compared to that of the infiltrating water. Also, because the preexisting pore water probably also came from the dry well, it is assumed that it has a contaminant concentration similar to that of the infiltrating water.

When water from the dry well reaches the water table, mixing with the water in the lens and spreading by advection and hydrodynamic dispersion dilutes the hypothetical contaminant. Hydrodynamic dispersion includes mechanical dispersion and molecular diffusion. In most cases, molecular diffusion is insignificant relative to mechanical dispersion (Zheng and Wang, 1999). In the conceptualization used in this study, molecular diffusion is considered to be negligible. The contaminant forms an ovoid plume with highest concentrations near the center (fig. 7A). The shape of the plume and concentrations in the saturated zone depend in part on how the infiltration pulse was drawn out as it passed through the unsaturated zone—a pulse that is more drawn out as a result of passing through a thicker unsaturated zone will produce a plume that is more elongate and has lower overall concentrations. Concentrations are attenuated as the plume spreads by advection and hydrodynamic dispersion as it migrates toward the coast with the regional flow of the freshwater lens. The rate of attenuation depends on the hydraulic properties of the aquifer and how much regional flow there is in the lens, but in general, concentrations diminish as the plume moves away from the dry well. When the plume has migrated far from the dry well as shown in block T4 in fig. 7A, the concentrations at the periphery of the plume have diminished so much that they don't register on the color scale, thus the plume appears smaller.

Numerical Models

The conceptual model used in this study has two components: (1) vertical unsaturated-zone flow, in which unsaturated-zone thickness and hydraulic properties determine the rate at which water and contaminants from the dry well are delivered to the freshwater lens, and (2) saturated-zone flow, in which the water and contaminants received from the unsaturated zone are incorporated into the flow of the freshwater lens and attenuate by advection and hydrodynamic dispersion (fig. 6).

Several computer programs are available for creating models to simulate flow and transport in the unsaturated and saturated zones, but most of these programs are more complex than required for the objectives of this study. Simulating transport of only one contaminant that is nonreactive and unaffected by evapotranspiration and by hydrodynamic dispersion in the unsaturated zone eliminated the need for a solute-transport model of the unsaturated zone. Therefore, the unsaturated-zone component of the modeling could be greatly simplified. The focus of the unsaturated-zone modeling was then reduced to determining how the infiltration pulse will be drawn out as it travels through the various thicknesses of unsaturated zone (fig. 6). The resulting recharge curves were then used as input to the saturated-zone models of flow and solute transport.

Each semi-generic model thus consisted of an unsaturated/saturated model pair; the saturated and unsaturated models were built and run separately but were related because they represented different parts of the same flow path from dry well to receiving water. Several semi-generic models were created to study the effect of dry wells in different hydrogeologic conditions, such as different unsaturated-zone thickness or different aquifer characteristics from one location to the next.

Flow in the Unsaturated Zone

Models of groundwater flow in the unsaturated zone were created using MODFLOW-2005 (Harbaugh, 2005) with the UZF1 package (Niswonger and others, 2006). MODFLOW-2005 is widely used to develop numerical finite-difference models of saturated groundwater flow; the UZF1 package is a module in MODFLOW-2005 for simulating unsaturated-zone flow. The UZF1 package uses a kinematic wave approximation that simulates one-dimensional (vertical) gravity-driven unsaturated flow (ignores negative potential gradients), which is consistent with the assumptions of the conceptual model for this study.

The basic form of the unsaturated-zone models created for this study is a tall rectangular box with a square horizontal surface representing a volume of the basaltic lava-flow aquifers that form most of the Island of Hawaiʻi (fig. 8). The surface is divided into nine equally sized cells: the center cell representing the dry well and the surrounding cells having a constant-head set at zero. The unsaturated zone of the model was not divided into multiple layers. In the model simulations, all water entering the dry well infiltrates vertically through the upper surface of the center dry-well cell; the UZF1 package does not simulate horizontal flow in the unsaturated zone. The model thus simulates the dry well as an area of infiltration rather than an injection well.

In the UZF1 package, the maximum infiltration rate (L^3/T) allowed through the dry-well cell is equal to the area of the cell (L^2) multiplied by K_v (L/T). As discussed above, the typical DPW dry well on the Island of Hawaiʻi has a diameter of only 5 ft, or a nominal infiltration area of about 20 ft^2, yet the dry wells are expected to accommodate as much as 5 ft^3/s of flow. Under such high-flow conditions, water entering the dry well must in reality flow horizontally through the walls of the dry wells and spread horizontally into the surrounding unsaturated rock until the area of infiltration is large enough for all of the water to flow vertically. For the models using the UZF1 package in this study, the infiltration area of the cell representing the dry well was determined by

$$A_{DW} = \frac{Q_{DW}}{K} , \qquad \text{(eq. 1)}$$

where A_{DW} is the infiltration area of the cell representing the dry well [L^2], and Q_{DW} is the flow rate into the dry well [L^3/T].

To simulate a condition where dry wells are absent (to represent the natural condition), infiltration was applied over a

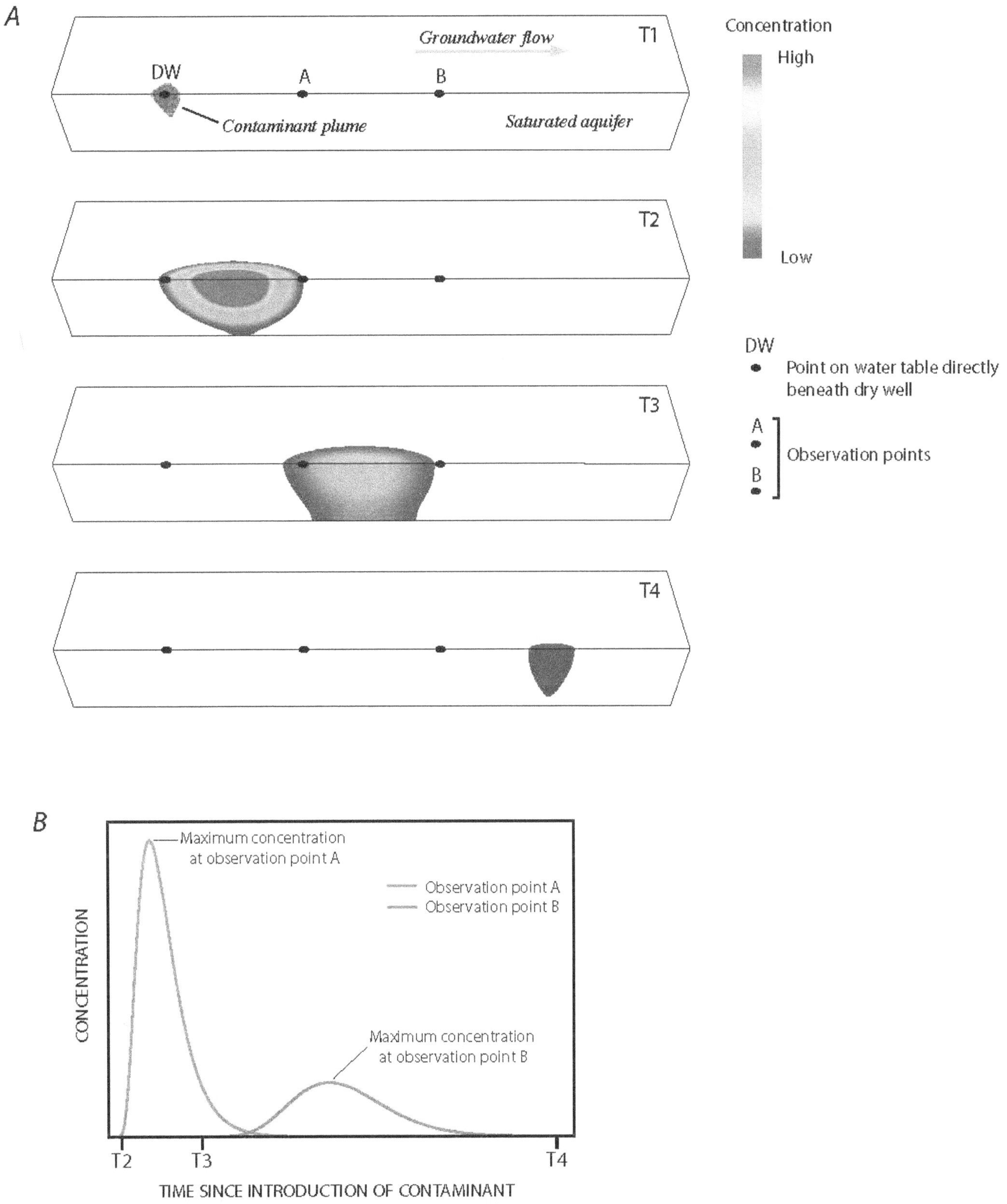

A

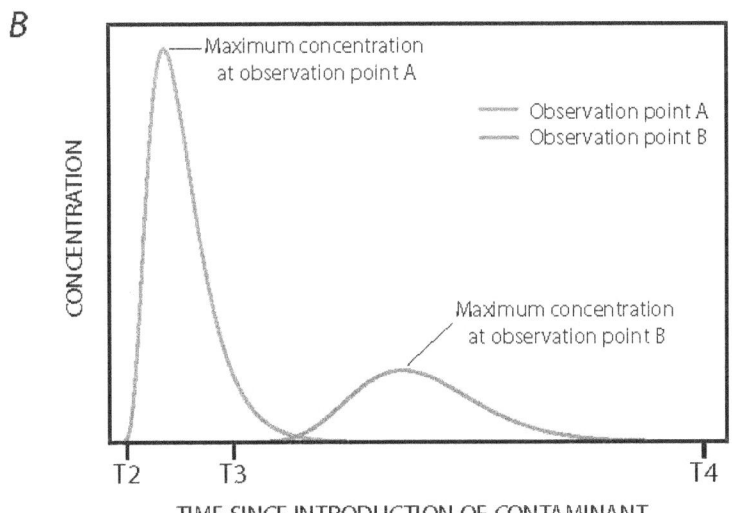

B

Figure 7.   *A*, Movement of a dry-well contaminant plume through a saturated aquifer with regional groundwater flow. Block diagrams are cut on a plane of symmetry to show one half of the plume in three dimensions. T1, T2, T3 and 4 indicate successively later time periods. *B*, Theoretical concentrations at various locations along the path of plume migration.

UNSATURATED-ZONE MODELS

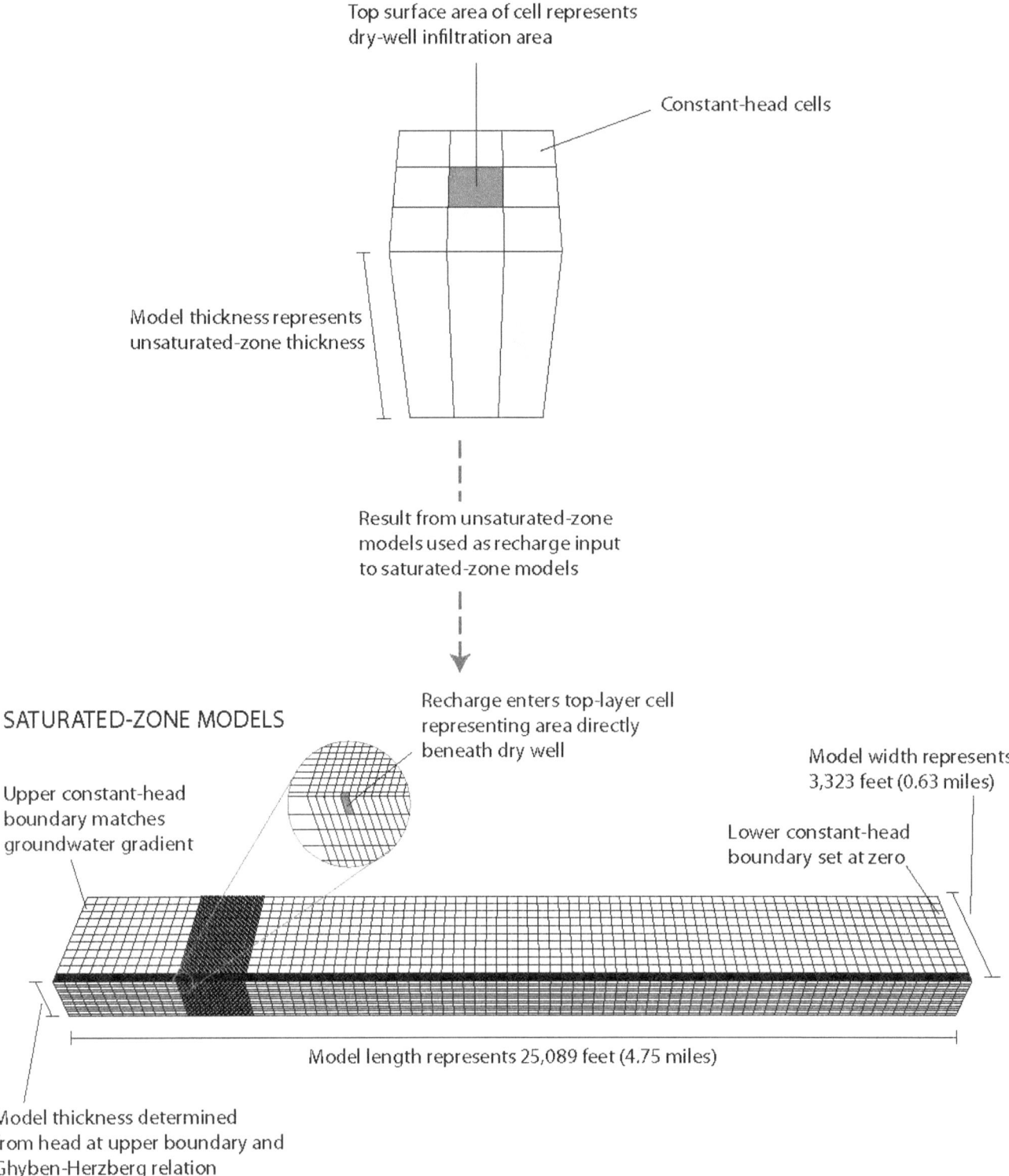

Top surface area of cell represents dry-well infiltration area

Constant-head cells

Model thickness represents unsaturated-zone thickness

Result from unsaturated-zone models used as recharge input to saturated-zone models

SATURATED-ZONE MODELS

Recharge enters top-layer cell representing area directly beneath dry well

Model width represents 3,323 feet (0.63 miles)

Upper constant-head boundary matches groundwater gradient

Lower constant-head boundary set at zero

Model length represents 25,089 feet (4.75 miles)

Model thickness determined from head at upper boundary and Ghyben-Herzberg relation

Figure 8.   General form of the unsaturated- and saturated-zone numerical models used in the study of the potential effects of dry wells on groundwater quality on the Island of Hawai'i.

broad area rather than focused in the small area of infiltration of a dry well. In this case, the infiltration area was assumed to be equal to the surface area needed to generate 5 ft³/s of runoff for 1 hour from the maximum hourly rainfall recorded at a nearby rain gage (see discussion in the Conceptual Model section, above).

Flow and Contaminant Transport in the Saturated Zone

The conceptual model for this study requires simulation of both groundwater flow and solute transport in the saturated zone. In this study, models of flow and transport in the saturated zone were created using SEAWAT Version 4 (Langevin and others, 2008). SEAWAT Version 4 couples MODFLOW-2000 (Harbaugh and others, 2000) with MT3DMS (Zheng and Wang, 1999) to create models capable of simulating three-dimensional, variable-density, saturated groundwater flow and solute transport. MODFLOW-2000, like MODFLOW-2005, is one of the series of versions that have expanded the analytical capabilities of MODFLOW beyond the groundwater-flow simulation of

the original version by McDonald and Harbaugh (1988) (see Harbaugh, 2005, for a history of MODFLOW). MT3DMS is a program for developing models that can simulate advection, hydrodynamic dispersion, and chemical reactions of contaminants in groundwater flow systems.

Model dimensions and boundary conditions.—In this study, the basic form of the saturated-zone models was an elongate rectangular box representing a volume of a lava-flow aquifer. The models had a top surface that represented an area 25,089 ft long and 3,323 ft wide (fig. 8, table 1). Each of the saturated-zone models had a single dry well at a distance of 3,349 to 3,373 ft from the upper constant head boundary (in these models, the upper constant head boundary represents the inland boundary). Model head gradients representing the regional groundwater gradients in the Kona and Hilo areas were created in the long direction of the models using constant-head boundaries. Head at the lower end of the gradient was set at 0 ft for all saturated-zone models. For Kona models, the upper end of the gradient was given a constant head of 3.27 ft based on the difference between average water levels in wells 4161-01 and 4160-02 (both near the Kona coast), which indicates a regional gradient of 0.7 ft/mi (Delwyn Oki, USGS,

Table 1. Aspects of the saturated-zone models of the semi-generic numerical models used to assess the effect of dry wells on solute transport on the Island of Hawaiʻi.

[All saturated-zone models were half-domain models]

Aspect of model	Kona models	Hilo models
Number of columns	133	113
Number of rows	19	15
Number of layers	14	33
Number of cells	35,378	55,935
Uppermost layer		
Top elevation (feet)	10	40
Bottom elevation (feet)	-1	-1
Thickness (feet)	11	41
Saturated thickness (feet)	1 to 4.3	1 to 27.8
Other layers		
Thickness of other layers (feet)	10.0	33.5
Elevation of bottom of lowermost layer (feet)	-131	-1,072
Dry well		
Location (layer, row, column)	1, 19, 16	1, 15, 15
Cell area (square feet)	547	1,335
Distance from upstream constant-head boundary node (feet)	3,349	3,373
Distance from downstream constant-head boundary node (feet)	21,437	21,414
Total model length (feet)	25,089	25,089
Total model width (feet)	3,323	3,323
Total model thickness (feet)	141	1,112
Distance between constant head nodes (feet)	24,786	24,786

written commun., 2010). For Hilo models, the upper end of the gradient was given a constant head of 26.80 ft based on the difference between average water levels in wells 4203-01 and 4304-01 (both near Hilo Bay), which indicates a regional gradient of 5.7 ft/mi (U.S. Geological Survey, 2010). The steeper gradient in Hilo compared to Kona is consistent with the higher rainfall (and therefore recharge and groundwater flux through the aquifer) in Hilo.

The bottom of the models and the sides along the long dimension are specified no-flow boundaries. The depth of the bottom was determined from the head in the upper constant-head boundary and the Ghyben-Herzberg relation:

$$Z_b = -40\ H_u,$$ (eq. 2)

where Z_b is the elevation of the bottom of the model and H_u is the head at the upper constant-head boundary. This is consistent with an assumption of no flow across the freshwater-saltwater transition zone, which is a common simplification in analyses of aquifers containing fresh water overlying salt water. The top of the saturated-zone models was set at an elevation of 10 ft for Kona and 40 ft for Hilo. This elevation is arbitrary and does not affect the outcome of the simulations (as discussed, the thickness of the unsaturated zone is accounted for by the separate unsaturated-zone models). Total thickness of the Kona saturated-zone models was 141 ft; total thickness of the Hilo saturated-zone models was 1,112 ft.

To increase computational efficiency and the speed of computer processing, the modeled area represented half of the flow and contaminant transport domain near the dry well. This procedure is commonly used in modeling when the domain is symmetrical across a vertical plane. In this case, the model is symmetrical across the vertical plane that runs through the dry well and is parallel to the regional flow direction. Because the saturated-zone model represents half the flow domain, the infiltration area of the dry well was equal to one-half the dry-well infiltration area of (A_{DW}) used in the corresponding unsaturated-zone model. The half-domain representation does not, however, affect the results of the simulation or conclusions of this study.

Model discretization.—The saturated-zone models were discretized (divided into small cells) for the numerical computation. The Kona models were discretized into 35,378 cells arranged in 133 columns, 19 rows, and 14 layers (table 1). The Hilo saturated-zone models were discretized into 55,935 cells arranged in 113 columns, 15 rows, and 33 layers. Most of the horizontal area of the saturated-zone models was coarsely discretized, with each cell having an area of about 300 by 300 ft. The area near the dry well, however, was more finely discretized, with most cells having an area equal to A_{DW} (see discussion of simulation of flow in the unsaturated zone, above). The saturated-zone models simulate the dry well as an area of recharge. The cell representing the dry well itself had an area of 0.5 A_{DW} (which also reduced recharge by a factor of 0.5) to account for the half-domain representation used in the saturated-zone models. The uppermost layer was 11 ft thick in the Kona models and 41 ft thick in the Hilo models.

Underlying layers were 10 ft thick in the Kona models and 33.5 ft thick in the Hilo models.

The time dimension was also discretized by dividing the simulation period into smaller time steps. Time discretization was important for converting output from the unsaturated-zone model to input for the saturated zone model, so it is discussed in greater detail below.

Linking the Unsaturated- and Saturated-Zone Models

Output from each unsaturated-zone model consisted of a time-varying recharge rate (fig 6). The shape of the recharge-time curve varied depending on the thickness of the unsaturated zone. In MODFLOW-based programs such as SEAWAT, time-varying recharge is specified using stress periods. Recharge must remain constant throughout each stress period, but can be changed from one stress period to the next. The more stress periods used, the more precisely the recharge curve from the unsaturated-zone model can be represented as input to the saturated-zone model. In most cases, however, the output from the unsaturated-zone models could be represented well with a few stress periods. In this study, the recharge curves from the unsaturated-zone models were sufficiently represented using 5 to 13 stress periods in the saturated-zone models. The first stress period in each simulation was used to achieve the initial steady-state conditions prior to the introduction of the recharge and contaminant from the dry well. From the second stress period to the end of the simulation, stress periods were further subdivided into smaller time steps to achieve greater numerical precision. Time steps ranged from 1 to 12 hours; shorter time steps in this range were used when increased precision was needed.

Simulating Contaminant Transport

Contaminant transport was simulated explicitly only in the saturated-zone models for this study. Starting from the second stress period, a constant hypothetical contaminant concentration of 100 concentration units (CU) (actual units for concentration are not relevant in this study) was specified in the recharge from the dry well. The simulated hypothetical contaminant was nonreactive (chemically conservative) and did not affect the density of the water in which it was dissolved. Recharge was the only source of the contaminant in the saturated model—water in the saturated zone had an initial concentration of zero. Specified variations in the recharge rate cause the contaminant-delivery rate to the saturated model to vary with time.

Key to meeting the objectives of this study is tracking the changes of the concentration of the hypothetical contaminant as it moves through the saturated-zone models. As discussed earlier, a contaminant dissolved in a pulse of water from a dry well forms a plume in the saturated aquifer (fig. 7A). Monitoring the contaminant concentration as the plume passes a point in the aquifer results in a concentration curve that rises as the front of the plume arrives, peaks, and subsequently declines as the plume moves away (fig. 7B). Because the contaminant spreads by advection and hydrodynamic dispersion as the plume moves away from the dry well, the maximum concentration in the plume decreases. The effect of contamination from the dry well can be assessed by monitoring the maximum concentration (concentration in the core of the plume) at various distances along the path of plume migration. In this study, concentrations along the migration path of the plume were monitored using the observation-point feature of SEAWAT. Observation points were specified along the flow path between the dry well and lower constant-head boundary in the uppermost layer of the model, where the concentrations within the plume core are highest. The simulated concentration in an observation point is an integration of the concentrations through the depth of the model cell representing the observation point. To ensure that the observation points monitored the highest part of the plume core where concentrations are greatest, the bottom of the uppermost layer of the model (which determines the bottom of the observation points) was set at –1 ft (table 1). This elevation is just 1 ft below the head at the lower constant-head boundary.

Input Data for the Numerical Models

In addition to the water levels and head gradients specified with the boundary conditions and the infiltration/recharge rates and contaminant concentrations discussed above, the numerical models in this study required specification of other hydrogeologic properties that affect groundwater flow and contaminant transport (table 2). The property values were selected from previous studies and existing data so that the resulting models are representative of the conditions that exist where dry wells are used on the Island of Hawai'i.

Hydraulic Properties of the Aquifer

Hydraulic conductivity.—Estimates of horizontal hydraulic conductivity (K_h) for the lava-flow aquifers in the flanks of volcanoes on the Island of Hawai'i vary widely. Oki (1999) cited several previous studies indicating that K_h ranges from 500 to 34,000 ft/d in flank aquifers on the Kona coast and used a value of 7,500 ft/d in a numerical model to obtain the best match with measured water levels. Underwood and others (1995) analyzed aquifer-test data from the northeast flank of the Kohala Volcano and estimated values of 610 to 2,700 ft/d for K_h; Oki (2002) found that using K_h values of 300 to 3,000 ft/d in a numerical model of the same area resulted in the best match with measured water levels. Whittier and others (2004) used K_h values from 39 to 8,200 ft/d to match water levels in volcano-flank aquifers in various locations on the island. The wide variability in estimated K_h can be attributed in part to the different methods of analysis, but much of the variability is likely related to variations in hydraulic properties from one

Table 2. Input data for the semi-generic numerical models used to assess the effect of dry wells on solute transport on the Island of Hawai'i.

Input data	Kona models	Hilo models
Dry-well infiltration (cubic feet per second for one hour)	5	5
Contaminant concentration in water from dry well (units unspecified)	100	100
Aquifer hydraulic properties		
Horizontal hydraulic conductivity (feet per day)	20,000	8,200
Vertical hydraulic conductivity (feet per day)	400	164
Porosity/saturated water content (dimensionless)	0.1	0.1
Specific yield (dimensionless)	0.055	0.055
Specific storage (1/feet)	0.000008	0.000008
Longitudinal dispersivity (feet)	250	250
Horizontal transverse dispersivity (feet)	25	25
Vertical transverse dispersivity (feet)	2.5	2.5
Additional input for unsaturated models		
Brooks-Corey exponent (dimensionless)	3.2	3.2
Initial water content (dimensionless)	0.045	0.045
Additional input for saturated/transport models		
Head gradient (feet per mile)	0.7	5.7
Constant head at upper boundary (feet)	3.27	26.80
Constant head at lower boundary (feet)	0	0

location to the next. In this study, a value of 20,000 ft/d was used in the Kona saturated- and unsaturated-zone models (table 2). This value is about midway in the range of K_h values in Kona and is consistent with groundwater gradients and tidal response in wells near the Kona coast (Delwyn Oki, USGS, oral commun., 2010). A value of 8,200 ft/d was used for K_h in the Hilo saturated and unsaturated models, which is consistent with the values used by Whittier and others (2004).

Values of K_v are usually much lower than K_h because aquifers formed by lava flows have a strongly layered character. Gingerich (2008) cited previous studies indicating that for lava-flow aquifers on Maui, K_v is tens to hundreds of times lower than K_h and used K_v values that were 1/67 to 1/800 of

K_h for the volcano-flank aquifers in a numerical groundwater model of West Maui. In a model of the flank of the East Maui shield volcano, Hunt (2007) used a value of K_v that was 1/200 of K_h. Rapid response to high-intensity rainfall indicates that the ratio of K_v to K_h is higher on the Island of Hawai'i, particularly in the Kona area. For example, data from Kaloko Monitor Well 3 in Kaloko-Honokōhau National Historical Park show concurrent abrupt changes in water levels, temperature, and specific conductance that indicate that water from the surface passed rapidly through the unsaturated zone to the water table (fig. 9). Hourly rainfall data from the nearby Kaloko-Honokōhau rain gage (fig. 3) shows a high-intensity rainstorm had started in the area a few hours prior to the

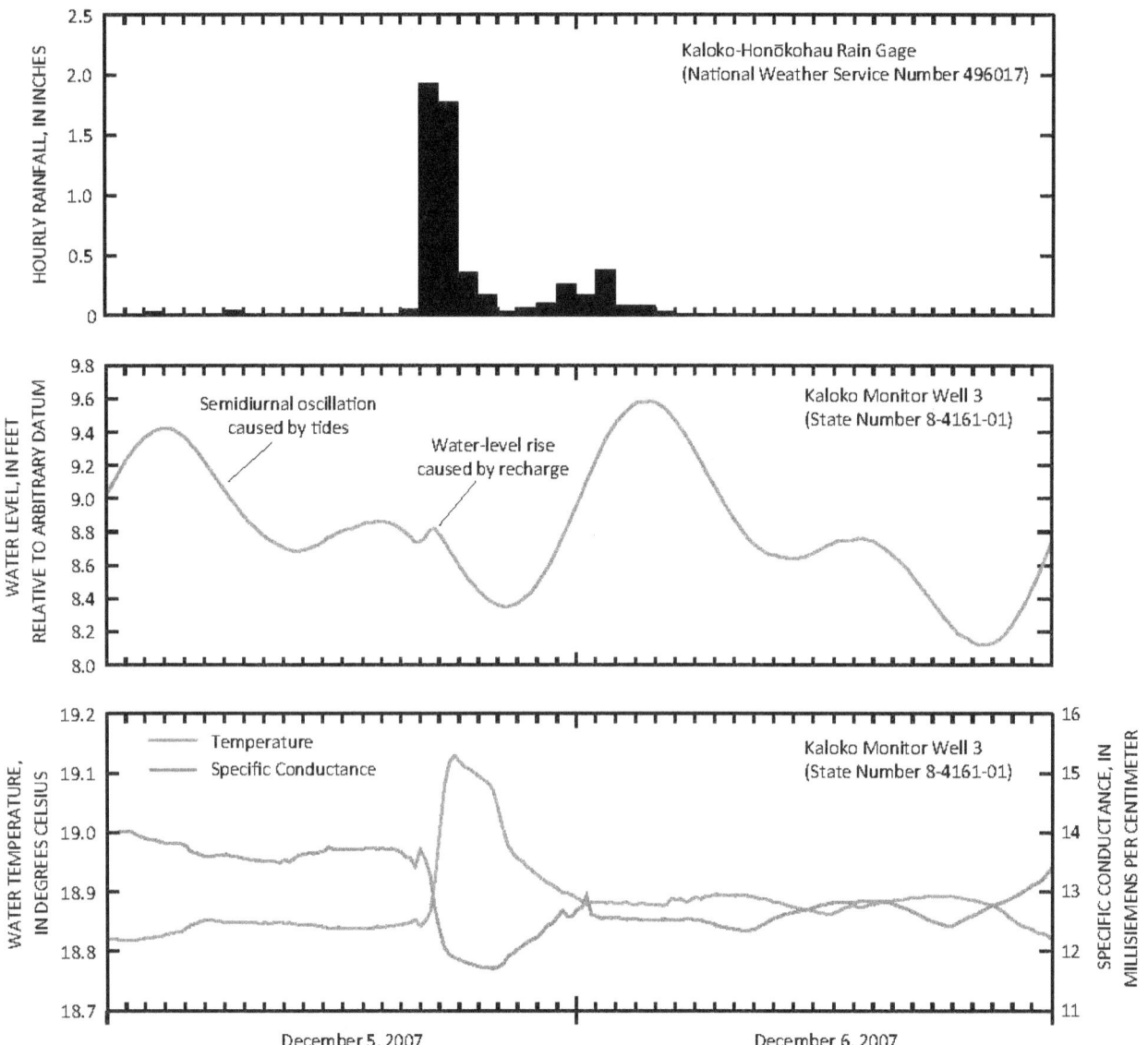

Figure 9.   Hourly rainfall from the Kaloko-Honokōhau gage and groundwater levels, temperature, and specific conductance in Kaloko Monitor Well 3, Kaloko-Honokōhau National Historical Park, Island of Hawai'i. (Rainfall data from Western Region Climate Center, 2010; unpublished monitor-well data from Kaloko-Honokōhau National Historical Park.)

changes recorded in the monitor well. These data indicate that water moves quickly through the 20 ft of unsaturated zone in this area, which is consistent with a high K_v. In this study, a value of 400 ft/d was used for K_v in the Kona saturated and unsaturated models, and a value of 164 ft/d was used in the Hilo saturated and unsaturated models (table 2). Both of these K_v values are 1/50 of their respective K_h values.

Porosity, specific yield, and specific storage.—Porosity, specific yield, and specific storage are hydrogeologic properties that relate to the storage capacity of aquifer systems. They also are important because they affect how long an infiltration pulse will take to travel through the unsaturated zone, how much that pulse will be drawn out as it flows through the unsaturated zone, and how quickly the saturated aquifer will respond to the increased recharge from the dry well. These property values, however, are poorly known for the basalt aquifers in Hawai'i.

For the numerical models in this study, estimates for hydrologic properties were determined by researching the range of possible values from previous hydrologic studies of the Hawaiian archipelago. Final values used in the models were determined by adjusting them (along with the Brooks-Corey exponent discussed later) in an unsaturated-zone model until the time it took the simulated infiltration pulse to reach the water table matched the short delay between rainfall recorded at the Kaloko-Honokōhau rain gage and the recharge evident in data from Kaloko Monitor Well 3 (fig. 9). The model used for this purpose had K_h and K_v values representative of the aquifers in Kona. The model had the same general structure as the unsaturated-zone models used in the semi-generic models (fig. 8) except for changes in the infiltration area, unsaturated-zone thickness, and time discretization. Most of the water recharging the aquifer near Kaloko Monitor Well 3 probably came from natural surface infiltration because the nearby area has no dry wells; therefore, a pulse of water equivalent to 5 ft³/s for 1 hour was specified in the unsaturated-zone model for this analysis and was applied over a large infiltration area (1.07×10^5 ft²) rather than focused in a dry well. The infiltration area was approximately equivalent to the area needed to generate 5 ft³/s with the highest 1-hour rainfall total from the USGS Kīholo rain gage discussed previously. The unsaturated-zone thickness was set at 20 ft to match the depth to water in Kaloko Monitor Well 3. The time dimension was discretized into finer time steps ranging from one minute to 0.1 day to allow better assessment of the lag between infiltration at the surface and recharge at the water table.

Comparison of the data from the Kaloko-Honokōhau rain gage and Kaloko Monitor Well 3 indicate that water traveled the 20 ft from the surface to the water table in less than 2 hours. The storage properties and Brooks-Corey exponent in the model were adjusted until the simulated lag between initiation of the infiltration pulse and arrival of water at the water table was also less than 2 hours (fig. 10). Resulting values for each of the storage parameters are discussed below.

Porosity is the proportion of the aquifer that consists of voids. More relevant for groundwater flow and contaminant

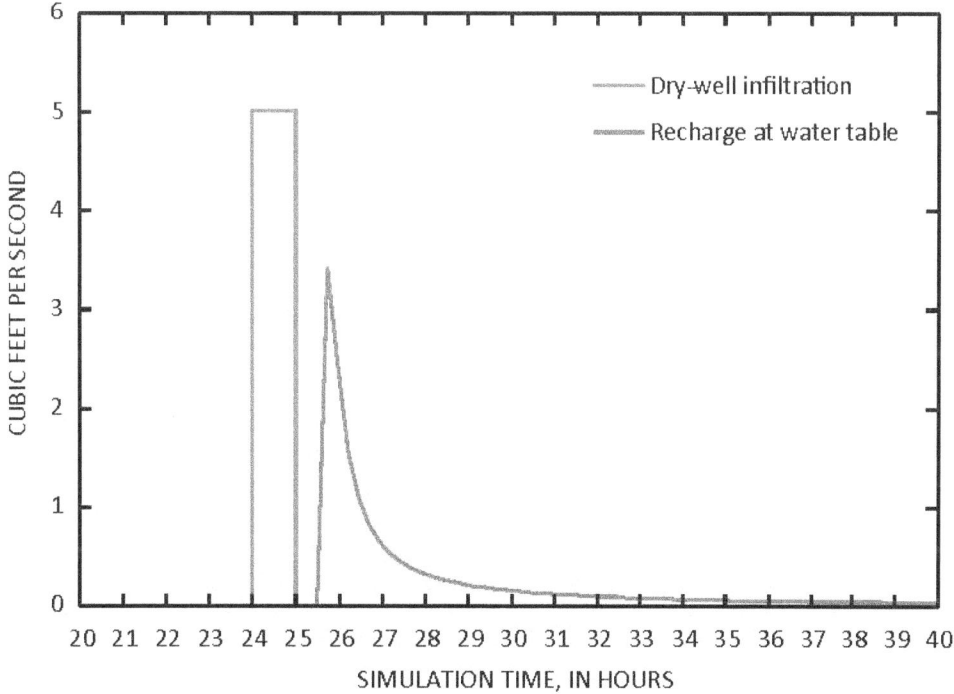

Figure 10.   Model-simulated lag between infiltration at dry well and recharge at water table resulting from parameters used in this study for the Kona area, Island of Hawai'i.

transport, however, is the effective porosity, or the proportion of the aquifer that consists of voids that are interconnected well enough to permit groundwater flow. Although estimates of porosity in basaltic lava flows on O'ahu range from about 0.05 to 0.5 (dimensionless), effective porosity may be lower by a factor of ten (Hunt, 1996). Recent investigations have used a wide range of values to adjust numerical groundwater models to match observed data. A value of 0.04 was used in a model of southern O'ahu by Gingerich and Voss (2005) and in a model of Kīhei, Maui, by Hunt (2007). Oki (2005) used a range of values from 0.04 to 0.1 in a model of O'ahu, and Gingerich (2008) used a value of 0.14 for a model of west Maui. A value of 0.1 was specified for porosity in all the numerical models for this study (table 2). This value is at the higher end of the range used in previous models, which is consistent with the premise that porosity reduction due to weathering is less likely in the younger aquifers on the Island of Hawai'i.

Specific yield is the volume of water that an unconfined aquifer releases from gravity drainage of the pore spaces; it is expressed as a volume of water per unit area per unit decline in head. Typically, only a portion of pore water can drain by gravity from the aquifer, so specific yield is less than effective porosity. Estimates of specific yield for basaltic lava-flow aquifers on O'ahu range between 0.01 to 0.42 (dimensionless), but most estimates are between about 0.05 and 0.10 (Hunt, 1996). Numerical models for O'ahu and Maui have used specific-yield values of 0.04 to 0.15 to simulate observed conditions (Souza and Voss, 1987; Oki, 2005; Gingerich and Voss, 2005; Gingerich, 2008). A value of 0.055 was used for specific yield in all numerical models for this study (table 2).

Specific storage is the volume of water that a unit volume of a saturated aquifer will release per unit decline in head. In contrast to specific yield, the water accounted for by specific storage is released without unsaturating the pores of the aquifer. The water comes from decompression of water and compaction of the matrix of the aquifer as a result of the reduction in head. A specific-storage value of 8×10^{-6} 1/ft was used in all of the models for this study (table 2). This value is consistent with values computed by Oki (2005) on the basis of water compressibility and estimates of the compressibility of O'ahu lava-flow aquifers reported by Souza and Voss (1987).

Dispersivity.—Because the saturated-zone models simulated contaminant transport in addition to groundwater flow, the models also required specification of dispersivity, a property that defines how a solute will disperse mechanically as it flows with groundwater through the porous aquifer. Dispersivity in the direction of flow is usually greater than dispersivity in the direction transverse (perpendicular) to flow. Also, vertical dispersivity may differ from horizontal dispersivity in layered aquifers such as the lava flow aquifers in Hawai'i. Most solute-transport models, including SEAWAT, therefore require input values for dispersivity in the horizontal longitudinal direction, as well as the horizontal and vertical transverse directions. Dispersion characteristics of basalt lava-flow aquifers in Hawai'i are poorly known. In all saturated-zone models in this study, values of 250 ft, 25 ft, and 2.5 ft were used for

horizontal longitudinal, horizontal transverse, and vertical transverse dispersivity, respectively (table 2). These values are similar to those used in previous studies to match the salinity distribution in the transition zone of numerical models with that measured in various locations in the Hawaiian archipelago (Souza and Voss, 1987; Oki, 2005; Gingerich, 2008).

Additional Input for the Unsaturated-Zone Models

The unsaturated-zone models required input values for two additional properties—saturated water content and initial water content—and one parameter—the Brooks-Corey exponent (table 2). The saturated water content for the unsaturated-zone models in this study was assumed to be the same as the porosity. The initial water content was assumed to be equal to the specific retention—the difference between the porosity and the specific yield. This assumption is consistent with the conceptual-model premise that water in the unsaturated zone moves downward only by the force of gravity and that once it is below the ground surface, it is unaffected by evapotranspiration.

The Brooks-Corey exponent is a parameter in the function used by UZF1 to determine how hydraulic conductivity varies with water content in the unsaturated zone (Niswonger and others, 2006). This parameter and the storage properties affect how long an infiltration pulse will take to travel through the unsaturated zone and how much the pulse will be drawn out as it flows through the unsaturated zone. As discussed above, final values of the storage properties and the Brooks-Corey exponent were determined by iterative adjustment until the simulated delay between the introduction of the infiltration pulse at the top of the unsaturated zone and its arrival at the water table matched observed monitoring-well and rainfall data (figs. 9 and 10). The value of 3.2 (dimensionless) resulting from this procedure was used for the Brooks-Corey exponent for all unsaturated-zone models in this study (table 2).

Results

Eleven semi-generic models were created to study the potential effects of dry wells on groundwater quality on the Island of Hawai'i (table 3). Parameter values in the semi-generic models were varied to study the effect of concentrating flow into a dry well compared to allowing the water to infiltrate naturally over a large area (dry well compared to no dry well), and how the effects of dry wells vary for different conditions likely to be present where dry wells exist on the Island of Hawai'i. All contaminant concentrations in this discussion of model results are expressed in concentration units (CU). Because the initial concentration of the infiltration water was 100 CU, the resulting concentrations in CU can also be directly converted to percent relative to the infiltration-water contaminant concentration (1 CU is equal to 1 percent).

Table 3. List of semi-generic models created to assess the effect of dry wells on groundwater quality on the Island of Hawaiʻi.

[Each semi-generic model consists of an unsaturated-zone model and a saturated-zone model]

Model name	Area represented	Thickness of unsaturated zone (feet)	Dry well simulated?
NDW50	Kona	50	No
Kona50	Kona	50	Yes
Kona700	Kona	700	Yes
Kona1000	Kona	1,000	Yes
Kona1600	Kona	1,600	Yes
Kona2000	Kona	2,000	Yes
Hilo50	Hilo	50	Yes
Hilo700	Hilo	700	Yes
Hilo1000	Hilo	1,000	Yes
Hilo1600	Hilo	1,600	Yes
Hilo2000	Hilo	2,000	Yes

Comparing Conditions With and Without Dry Well

Two of the semi-generic models were compared to study how directing storm runoff into a dry well affects groundwater quality in comparison to allowing the water to naturally infiltrate over a large area. Both models had an unsaturated-zone thickness of 50 ft, hydraulic properties and head gradients representative of Kona aquifers, and an infiltration rate of 5 ft^3/s for 1 hour. To simulate the condition with a dry well, infiltration in the unsaturated-zone model of one semi-generic model (Kona50 in table 3) was concentrated in an area of 1.08×10^3 ft^2, which represents the A_{DW} for a dry well in an aquifer having a K_v representative of Kona aquifers. To simulate the natural condition (no dry well), infiltration for the unsaturated-zone model of another semi-generic model (NDW50) was spread over an area of 1.07×10^5 ft^2. This area is approximately equivalent to the area needed to generate 5 ft^3/s from the highest 1-hour rainfall total from the USGS Kiholo rain gage.

Table 4 and figure 11A show the model-simulated maximum concentration in the contaminant plume that forms when water and contaminants from the dry well or natural infiltration area reach the saturated aquifer, and how the concentration changes as the plume moves through the saturated aquifer driven by the regional groundwater flow. In the simulation of the dry-well conditions, maximum contaminant concentration in the saturated aquifer directly beneath the dry well is 53.7 CU, or 53.7 percent of the concentration in the infiltration water. In contrast, the simulation of natural conditions

indicates that maximum contaminant concentration directly beneath the infiltration area is 6.8 CU, or 6.8 percent of the concentration in the infiltration water.

In both the dry-well and natural conditions, concentrations diminish with distance from the dry well (fig. 11A). In the simulation of the dry-well condition, maximum concentration is about 54 CU when the plume is centered directly beneath the dry well but less than 4 CU when the plume center has traveled 299 ft downgradient from the dry well (table 4). In the natural condition, the decline in simulated plume concentration with distance from the infiltration area is more gradual—maximum concentration is about 7 CU when the plume center is directly beneath the center of the infiltration area and declines very gradually over the next 100 ft because the plume is still beneath the larger infiltration area. When the plume passes from beneath the infiltration area, the maximum concentration declines more rapidly and is about 1 CU at a horizontal distance of 398 ft downgradient from the center of the infiltration area. At greater horizontal distances from the infiltration area, the concentration curves of the dry well and natural conditions converge. Concentrations in both

Table 4. Results from semi-generic models with and without a dry well with a 50-foot-thick unsaturated zone and hydraulic properties representative of aquifers in the Kona area, Island of Hawaiʻi.

[<, less than]

Horizontal distance downgradient from dry well/infiltration area (feet)	Simulated maximum concentration for indicated condition (concentration units)	
	With dry well	Natural (no dry well)
0	53.7	6.8
33	40.9	6.7
66	28.8	6.4
100	18.1	5.8
166	8.9	3.1
232	5.1	1.9
299	3.3	1.4
398	1.9	0.9
531	1.1	0.6
697	0.7	0.4
930	0.4	0.3
1,361	0.2	0.1
2,764	0.1	0.1
6,679	< 0.1	< 0.1
12,100	< 0.1	< 0.1
21,136	< 0.1	< 0.1

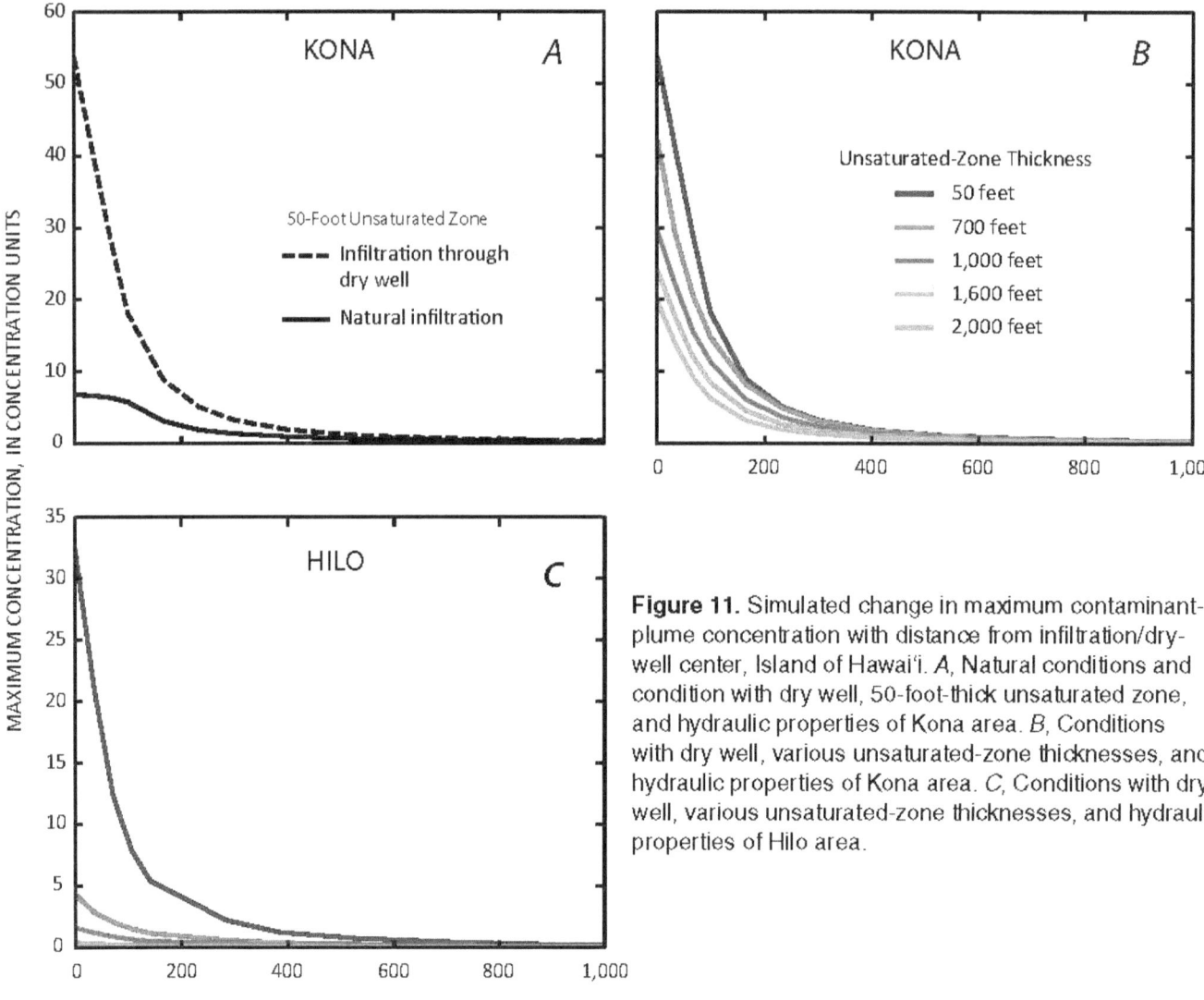

Figure 11. Simulated change in maximum contaminant-plume concentration with distance from infiltration/dry-well center, Island of Hawai'i. *A,* Natural conditions and condition with dry well, 50-foot-thick unsaturated zone, and hydraulic properties of Kona area. *B,* Conditions with dry well, various unsaturated-zone thicknesses, and hydraulic properties of Kona area. *C,* Conditions with dry well, various unsaturated-zone thicknesses, and hydraulic properties of Hilo area.

simulations were about 0.1 CU at a distance of 2,764 ft down-gradient from the infiltration sites.

Variations Due to Unsaturated-Zone Thickness, Horizontal Distance, and Location

Ten semi-generic models were created to assess variability in contaminant concentrations resulting from the thickness of the unsaturated zone between the dry well and the water table, horizontal distance from the dry well, and whether the dry wells are in the Kona or Hilo area (table 3). Five unsaturated-zone thicknesses were tested: 50 ft, 700 ft, 1,000 ft, 1,600 ft, and 2,000 ft. These thicknesses span the range of unsaturated zones beneath 85 percent of the DPW dry wells listed by Izuka and others (2009). Observation points in the saturated-zone model were used to assess variability

with horizontal distance. Variability due to location on the island was assessed by specifying hydraulic properties and head gradient representative of aquifers in the Kona area for half of the semi-generic models and hydraulic properties and head gradient representative of aquifers in the Hilo area for the other half.

Kona Area.—An infiltration rate of 5 ft^3/s for 1 hour was specified for dry wells in the Kona area semi-generic models. This infiltration was applied to an unsaturated-zone model area of 1.08×10^3 ft^2, which represents the A_{DW} for a dry well in an aquifer having a K_v representative of Kona aquifers. Table 5 and figure 11B show that the model-simulated maximum concentration of the contaminant plume that forms directly beneath the dry well is inversely proportional to the thickness of the unsaturated zone. Maximum concentrations directly beneath the dry wells are 53.7, 42.0, 29.6, 24.2, and 19.8 CU when the unsaturated zone is 50, 700, 1,000, 1,600, and 2,000 ft thick, respectively.

Maximum concentrations decline as the plume migrates away from the area beneath the dry well (fig. 11*B*). The differences among the curves in figure 11*B* are larger near the dry well, and diminish with distance from the dry well. At a horizontal distance of 232 ft downgradient from the dry well, the maximum concentrations have all declined below 6.0 CU, and at a distance of 2,764 ft, the concentrations are all 0.1 CU or less (table 5).

Hilo Area.—Dry wells in the Hilo-area semi-generic models were also given an infiltration rate of 5 ft³/s for 1 hour (table 2). A value of 2.63×10^3 ft² was used for A_{DW} in the unsaturated-zone models to represent the infiltration area of a dry well in an aquifer having a K_v representative of Hilo aquifers. As in the Kona models, maximum simulated contaminant concentrations in the saturated zone below the dry well are higher for thinner unsaturated zones and lower for thicker unsaturated zones (fig. 11*C*). However, concentrations in the models of the Hilo area are lower than comparable models of the Kona area. Maximum concentrations directly under the dry well in the Hilo models are 32.4, 4.2, 1.6, 0.3, and 0.2 CU when the unsaturated zone is 50, 700, 1,000, 1,600, and 2,000 ft thick, respectively (table 6). As in the models of the Kona area, maximum plume concentrations diminish quickly with horizontal

distance from the dry well. At a horizontal distance of 210 ft downgradient from the dry well, the maximum concentrations in the Hilo models have all declined below 4.0 CU, and at a distance of 2,755 ft, the concentrations are all less than 0.1 CU.

Discussion

All of the semi-generic models in this study indicate that mixing of contaminated water from the surface with contaminant-free water in the saturated aquifer immediately reduces the contaminant concentration. How much the concentration is reduced depends on the rate at which the infiltration water and its contaminant are introduced as recharge to the saturated aquifer. This rate, in turn, depends on whether the infiltration is focused in a small area (such as in a dry well) or a large area (such as under natural conditions), the hydraulic properties of the aquifer, and the thickness of the unsaturated zone. Contaminant concentrations diminish further as the contaminant plume is incorporated into the regional groundwater flow and migrates from beneath the dry well.

Table 5.   Results from semi-generic models with various unsaturated-zone thicknesses and hydraulic properties representative of aquifers in the Kona area, Island of Hawai'i.

[<, less than]

Horizontal distance downgradient from dry well (feet)	Simulated maximum concentration for indicated unsaturated-zone thickness (concentration units)				
	50 feet	**700 feet**	**1,000 feet**	**1,600 feet**	**2,000 feet**
0	53.7	42.0	29.6	24.2	19.8
33	40.9	29.1	22.0	17.5	13.8
66	28.8	20.5	15.5	12.0	9.2
100	18.1	14.7	11.3	8.4	6.2
166	8.9	8.2	6.1	4.5	3.2
232	5.1	4.9	3.6	2.7	1.9
299	3.3	3.1	2.4	1.8	1.3
398	1.9	1.8	1.4	1.1	0.8
531	1.1	1.1	0.8	0.7	0.5
697	0.7	0.6	0.5	0.4	0.3
930	0.4	0.4	0.3	0.2	0.2
1,361	0.2	0.2	0.1	0.1	0.1
2,764	0.1	< 0.1	< 0.1	< 0.1	< 0.1
6,679	< 0.1	< 0.1	< 0.1	< 0.1	< 0.1
12,100	< 0.1	< 0.1	< 0.1	< 0.1	< 0.1
21,136	< 0.1	< 0.1	< 0.1	< 0.1	< 0.1

Table 6.   Results from semi-generic models with various unsaturated-zone thicknesses and hydraulic properties representative of aquifers in the Hilo area, Island of Hawai'i.

[<, less than]

Horizontal distance downgradient from dry well (feet)	Simulated maximum concentration for indicated unsaturated-zone thickness (concentration units)				
	50 feet	700 feet	1,000 feet	1,600 feet	2,000 feet
0	32.4	4.2	1.6	0.3	0.2
35	21.1	2.8	1.2	0.3	0.1
70	12.3	2.0	0.9	0.2	0.1
105	7.9	1.5	0.6	0.2	0.1
140	5.3	1.1	0.5	0.1	0.1
210	3.8	0.9	0.4	0.1	0.1
281	2.2	0.6	0.3	0.1	< 0.1
386	1.2	0.3	0.2	0.1	< 0.1
526	0.7	0.2	0.1	< 0.1	< 0.1
702	0.4	0.2	0.1	< 0.1	< 0.1
912	0.2	0.1	0.1	< 0.1	< 0.1
1,368	0.1	< 0.1	< 0.1	< 0.1	< 0.1
2,755	< 0.1	< 0.1	< 0.1	< 0.1	< 0.1
6,671	< 0.1	< 0.1	< 0.1	< 0.1	< 0.1
12,092	< 0.1	< 0.1	< 0.1	< 0.1	< 0.1
21,127	< 0.1	< 0.1	< 0.1	< 0.1	< 0.1

Simulated Effects of Dry Wells

Model results indicate that the presence of a dry well could substantially increase contaminant concentrations in the underlying saturated aquifer relative to natural conditions, even if the concentrations in the infiltration water are the same for both simulations (fig. 11, table 4). Simulated concentrations directly beneath a dry well were nearly eight times higher than the simulated concentrations directly beneath a broad infiltration area representing the natural condition. Because infiltration in the dry-well condition is concentrated in a small area, the head differential driving the unsaturated flow is high and the infiltration pulse moves downward quickly. The pulse is only slightly drawn out before it reaches the saturated aquifer, therefore a large volume of water and contaminants are delivered in a short time (fig. 12A). In contrast, infiltration in the natural condition is spread over a much larger area, so the head differential driving the unsaturated flow is less and the infiltration pulse moves downward more slowly. The pulse becomes more drawn out, therefore water and contaminants are delivered to the saturated aquifer more gradually. Spreading the infiltration over a large area also allows the contaminants to mix with a larger volume of water in the saturated aquifer.

When dry wells route contaminated runoff through the groundwater system, model results indicate that the thicker the unsaturated zone, the lower the concentrations in the saturated aquifer (fig. 11, tables 5 and 6,). Where the unsaturated zone is thin, the infiltration pulse is only slightly drawn out before it reaches the saturated aquifer, therefore a large volume of water and contaminants are delivered in a short time (fig. 12B,C). Where the unsaturated zone is thick, however, the infiltration pulse is more drawn out, so water and contaminants are delivered to the saturated aquifer more gradually. Eighty-nine percent of the DPW dry wells listed in the inventory by Izuka and others (2009) have unsaturated-zone thicknesses of 50 ft or more; 26 percent have unsaturated-zone thicknesses greater than 700 ft.

In all situations simulated by the semi-generic models, concentrations decline quickly as the plume migrates from the dry well (fig. 11, tables 4–6). Distinction between results from the different simulated unsaturated-zone thicknesses also diminishes with distance from the dry well. In all cases simulated, the maximum concentrations at a distance of about 700 ft downgradient from the dry wells were less than 1 percent of the concentration in the infiltration water. At a distance of about 0.5 mi downgradient from the dry well, the simulated maximum concentrations were all 0.1 percent or less of the concentration

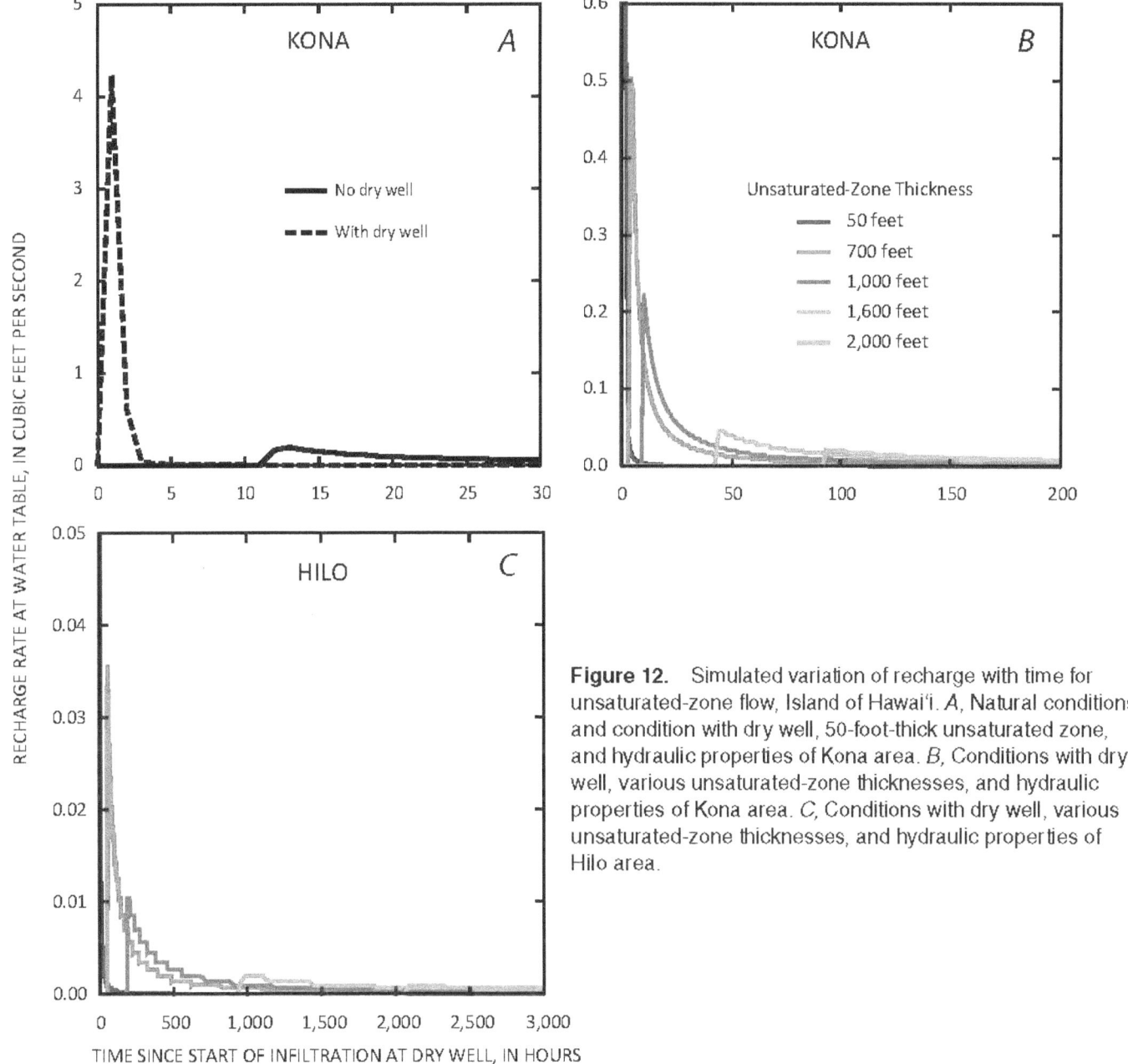

Figure 12. Simulated variation of recharge with time for unsaturated-zone flow, Island of Hawai'i. *A*, Natural conditions and condition with dry well, 50-foot-thick unsaturated zone, and hydraulic properties of Kona area. *B*, Conditions with dry well, various unsaturated-zone thicknesses, and hydraulic properties of Kona area. *C*, Conditions with dry well, various unsaturated-zone thicknesses, and hydraulic properties of Hilo area.

in the infiltration water. Because the models simulate a nonreactive, nondecaying contaminant, all of the simulated concentration reduction is caused by hydrodynamic dispersion and advection only. Decay and reaction can, however, reduce concentrations of some types of contaminants even further.

Differences from one location to the next, such as the differences in hydraulic properties and regional head gradients between aquifers in the Kona and Hilo areas, also affect concentrations in the saturated aquifer directly beneath the dry well and the rate at which the contaminants diminish as the plume migrates away from beneath the dry well. In general, the maximum concentrations in the Hilo models are not as high as in Kona models having comparable unsaturated-zone thicknesses.

The lower value of K_V used in the Hilo models results in an infiltration pulse that is more drawn out with time compared to that of Kona models (compare fig. 12*B* and 12*C*); thus, water and contaminants recharge the saturated aquifer more gradually in Hilo than in Kona. The groundwater flux through the Hilo aquifer is also greater than in Kona. Even though K_H in Hilo is lower than it is in Kona, the steeper regional head gradient in Hilo results in higher groundwater flux. The higher flux is consistent with the wetter climate in Hilo relative to Kona (fig. 2). The combination of more gradual recharge from the unsaturated zone and greater groundwater flux in the saturated zone results in lower overall concentrations in the Hilo models relative to comparable Kona models.

Sensitivity of Results to Uncertainties in Hydrogeologic Properties and Model Parameters

The results described above are based on hydrogeologic-property values that were considered representative of aquifers on the Island of Hawai'i as described in the cited literature. For some properties, however, other values may be plausible. To test the sensitivity of the semi-generic models to the range of plausible values, one of the semi-generic models, Kona700 (table 3), was used as a base case, and several models were created in which the values of selected properties and parameters were varied singly or in combination. The results of these tests were compared to the base case to evaluate how parameter uncertainty may affect conclusions about the contaminant concentrations discussed in this report.

Properties tested in the sensitivity analysis were head gradient, dispersivity, infiltration rate at the dry well, K_H, K_V, porosity and specific yield, and specific storage (table 7). Each property value was varied by multiplying the value in the base case by factors of 0.5 and 2.0. Varying specific storage over this range had very little effect on the resultant concentrations. Varying the infiltration rate at the dry well, K_H, and the head gradient had a larger effect, but the effects are still relatively small and primarily affect the area within a few hundred feet of the dry well. The effect of varying the infiltration rate was also relatively small, in part because a change in the infiltration rate requires, and is partly mitigated by, a change in the A_{DW} (eq. 1).

The sensitivity analysis indicates that the semi-generic model results are most sensitive to variations in values for K_V, dispersivity, and porosity and specific yield (table 7). Although

Table 7. Results from sensitivity tests of hydrogeologic properties and model parameters used in the semi-generic model with a 700-foot-thick unsaturated zone and hydraulic properties representative of aquifers in the Kona area (model Kona700), Island of Hawai'i.

[ft, feet]

Change in test parameter value relative to values in model Kona700	Difference in maximum concentrations between sensitivity test and model Kona700, for indicated horizontal distance from dry well (concentration units)						
	0 ft	100 ft	232 ft	531 ft	1,361 ft	2,764 ft	21,136 ft
Head gradient							
Multiply by 0.5	6.1	0.1	0.0	0.0	0.0	0.0	0.0
Multiply by 2.0	-6.5	-0.4	-0.2	-0.1	0.0	0.0	0.0
Dispersivities							
Multiply by 0.5	17.6	6.9	2.4	0.8	0.2	0.1	0.0
Multiply by 2.0	-14.0	-4.6	-1.5	-0.4	-0.1	0.0	0.0
Dry-well infiltration							
Multiply by 0.5	-5.0	-4.8	-2.2	-0.5	-0.1	0.0	0.0
Multiply by 2.0	3.4	5.5	3.1	0.9	0.2	0.1	0.0
Horizontal hydraulic conductivity							
Multiply by 0.5	1.9	0.5	0.1	0.0	0.0	0.0	0.0
Multiply by 2.0	-3.3	-1.2	-0.5	-0.1	0.0	0.0	0.0
Vertical hydraulic conductivity							
Multiply by 0.5	-16.5	-5.4	-1.9	-0.3	0.0	0.0	0.0
Multiply by 2.0	17.9	1.1	0.1	0.0	0.0	0.0	0.0
Porosity and specific yield							
Multiply by 0.5	16.5	8.9	3.3	1.0	0.2	0.1	0.0
Multiply by 2.0	-18.8	-7.2	-2.9	-0.6	-0.1	0.0	0.0
Specific storage							
Multiply by 0.5	0.0	0.0	0.0	0.0	0.0	0.0	0.0
Multiply by 2.0	0.0	0.0	0.0	0.0	0.0	0.0	0.0

higher and lower values for these parameters are plausible for the basalts on the Island of Hawai'i, the values used in this study were considered most representative for the Island of Hawai'i on the basis of values reported in the literature. The discrepancies between the results of the sensitivity tests and model Kona700 are greatest at the location directly beneath the dry well but decline quickly with distance from the dry well. At 531 ft, the discrepancies are near or less than 1 CU, and at 2,764 ft, they are all equal to or less than 0.1 CU. Thus, the uncertainty associated with the plausible values tested in the sensitivity analysis primarily affects the area within a few hundred feet of the dry well.

Using Simulation Results to Estimate Effect of Dry Wells on Receiving Waters

The objective of this study was to provide results that are relevant to all dry wells on the Island of Hawai'i. The semi-generic approach was used so that results would not be restricted to any one area. The results from the models can be used to assess how contaminants entering a dry well may affect receiving waters in a variety of situations on the Island of Hawai'i. Suppose, for example, that a dry well with a 50-ft unsaturated zone is situated 500 ft upgradient from a receiving water of concern in the Kona area. A plot of data from table 5, focused on the area near a horizontal distance of 500 ft from the dry well, indicates that the concentration of a nonreactive contaminant at 500 ft downgradient from the dry well would have diminished to about 1.3 percent of the original concentration in the dry-well water (fig. 13). If a specific contaminant with a specified concentration is known to be in the water entering the dry well, its concentration in receiving waters located 500 ft away can be estimated by multiplying the concentration of the contaminant in the dry-well water by 0.013. Although it was beyond the scope of this study to determine contaminant concentrations for water entering dry wells on the Island of Hawai'i, it is likely that the contaminants would include those typically found in road runoff such as cadmium, chromium, copper, iron, lead, nickel, and zinc (Grant and others, 2003; De Carlo and others, 2004; Göbel and others, 2007; Presley and others, 2008). Wolff and Wong (2008) reported dissolved concentrations as high as 4.7 µg/L for chromium, 8.6 µg/L for copper, and 39 µg/L for zinc in samples from a storm drain receiving runoff from the H3 Interstate freeway in Hālawa Valley, O'ahu. If water containing these concentrations entered the dry well described here, the concentrations at the receiving water would be 6.1×10^{-2}, 1.1×10^{-1}, and 5.1×10^{-1} µg/L, respectively, assuming the metals were nonreactive. All of these metals, as well as most contaminants typically found in urban runoff, however, react to some degree with the aquifer or particulate matter carried in the water; these reactions commonly reduce the dissolved concentrations of these contaminants (De Carlo and others, 2004; Grant and others, 2003).

Approximations can also be obtained for unsaturated-zone thicknesses other than those modeled. For example, 63

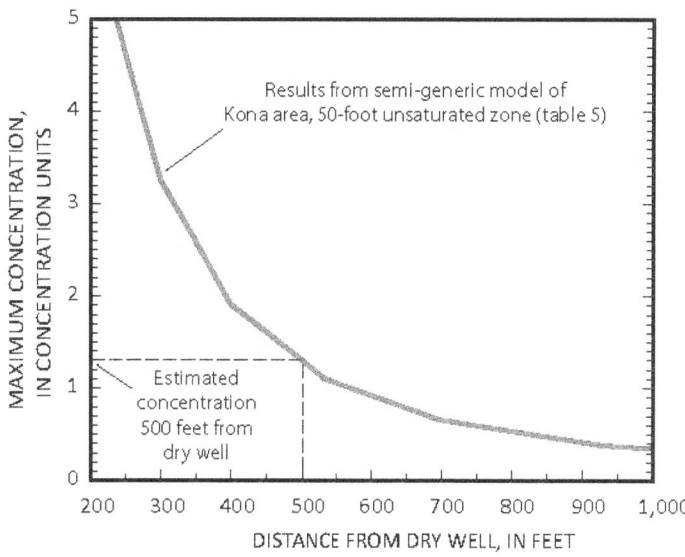

Figure 13. Simulated change in maximum contaminant-plume concentration with distance from beneath a dry well for a model with 50-foot-thick unsaturated zone and properties representative of aquifers in the Kona area, Island of Hawai'i Dashed line shows how the concentration can be estimated at a horizontal distance of 500 feet from the dry well.

percent of DPW dry wells have unsaturated zone thicknesses between 50 and 700 ft (Izuka and others, 2009). Approximations for these dry wells would lie between the curves for 50- and 700-ft-thick unsaturated zones. Because the concentration curves from the different unsaturated zone thicknesses converge a few hundred feet horizontally from the dry well (fig. 11), the significance of unsaturated zone thickness becomes less at greater distances.

The Kona and Hilo areas represent the range of conditions likely to be encountered where dry wells are used on the Island of Hawai'i. Hilo and Kona also encompass most of the DPW dry wells on the island (fig. 1). To use the simulation results to assess concentrations for locations other than Kona and Hilo, better assessment would be obtained by using results from the semi-generic models having the most similar conditions (such as climate, hydrogeologic properties, regional groundwater gradient). For example, dry wells in the Puna District (fig. 1) lie in an area with a climate more similar to Hilo than to Kona, therefore a more accurate assessment can be obtained by using results from the model of the Hilo area.

Study Limitations

The basis of the semi-generic model approach used in this study is the generalization of simulated conditions. Generalization of values for model input parameters was necessary to meet the study objectives of making the results applicable to all wells on the Island of Hawaiʻi. Generalization, however, also makes the results nonspecific to any particular location. The foregoing discussions show how the results of this study can be easily used to assess the potential effect of contaminants entering any specific dry well on receiving waters on the island, but the accuracy of the analysis is limited by the generalized nature of the models.

Although the range in values for hydrogeologic properties used in this study was wide enough to encompass most conditions indicated in the previous studies of the Island of Hawaiʻi, especially those in Kona and Hilo where most DPW dry wells are currently located, it is possible that a few dry wells are in areas where other values would be more representative. Results of this study are most relevant to areas having conditions that are generally similar to those represented by the model.

The semi-generic models represent a homogeneous, high-permeability aquifer with hydrogeologic properties representative of basaltic lava-flow aquifers on the Island of Hawaiʻi. The models do not consider the effect of surface soil or sedimentary rocks, low-permeability geologic structures such as dikes or other intrusive bodies, or buried soil and ash layers. The models also do not consider preferential flow paths (features of extremely high conductivity) such as lava tubes. These effects were not addressed in this study because they are primarily local and cannot be generalized to meet the objectives of this study.

The difference in hydraulic properties between the Hilo and Kona areas was simulated by using different values for K_V, K_H, and the groundwater gradient. It is possible that storage properties and the Brooks-Corey exponent may also be different between Kona and Hilo. However, only data from the Kona area was available for determining the storage properties using the procedures discussed above.

The analysis in this study assumes a single infiltration event of 5 ft^3/s for 1 hour and the concentration does not vary in that time. In reality, runoff produced by storms is likely to result in infiltration pulses and concentrations that are more complex than assumed here. Multiple storms can result in multiple infiltration pulses in the unsaturated zone, each having different contaminant concentrations. Water from these infiltration pulses can merge in the unsaturated zone. Concentrations can vary even within the infiltration of runoff from a single storm. For example, contaminant concentrations in runoff are commonly higher earlier in a runoff event than later (De Carlo and Anthony, 2002; De Carlo and others, 2004; Wolff and Wong, 2008).

Only a single well was simulated in the semi-generic models of this study. Most dry wells on the Island of Hawaiʻi, however, are clustered together in urban developments. Plumes from multiple dry wells and different infiltration events can merge, which can result in concentrations that are higher than indicated by the models and analyses in this study. It was also assumed that the dry well is the only source of contamination, but contamination can come from other sources.

The study results are based on an unspecified hypothetical nonreactive, nondecaying contaminant and diminish only

by advection and hydrodynamic dispersion. All contaminants are subject to advection and hydrodynamic dispersion. Some contaminants, however, also undergo decay or adsorb to the aquifer matrix or particles suspended in the water; dissolved concentrations of these contaminants may be lower than indicated in this study.

This study assumes that the contaminants are dissolved in the water infiltrating the ground through dry wells. As discussed previously, because many contaminants associated with roadside runoff will partition onto solids rather than remain dissolved in water, dissolved concentrations can be lower than indicated by the models in this study. However, because these contaminants may be transported as particulates, total concentrations (contaminant carried both in solution and attached to suspended particles) can be substantially higher than dissolved concentrations (see for example, data for the H3 storm drain described by Wolff and Wong, 2008). Many of the particles suspended in flowing water will probably settle out when flow energy diminishes in the dry well, but some small particles (for example colloidal-scale particles) may not settle out even when the flow energy is low (Breault and Granato, 2000; Grant and others, 2003). Whether a contaminant adsorbed onto particles will be detrimental depends on the nature of the receiving water. Sediments accumulated at the bottom of dry wells are also likely to contain contaminants. The accumulated sediments can act as a contaminant sorbent under some conditions and a contaminant source under other conditions (Mikkelsen and others, 1996). Periodic cleaning of sediments from dry wells to maintain performance may partially mitigate the effect of dry wells on groundwater quality.

The results of this study are expressed in terms of maximum concentration in the migrating contaminant plume. Although this approach describes the highest concentrations likely to occur at the receiving waters, it does not indicate the length of time the receiving water is likely to be exposed to this concentration. As shown in figure 7B, the concentration at a given point (such as a receiving water) downgradient from the dry well is near its maximum for only a brief period. A lower concentration, however, will be equaled or exceeded over a longer period. If the lower concentration is considered detrimental to the receiving water, the longer exposure may be of concern.

In the comparison of natural conditions to the condition with dry wells, the "natural condition" simulated in the models assumes that none of the water runs off to the ocean through surface-water routes such as streams. This may not be an accurate assumption in some areas of the Island of Hawaiʻi, such as in the Hilo area where natural surface drainage systems are well developed. In these areas, the "natural condition" may be more accurately conceptualized as having surface-water drainage that provides a more direct route (compared to dry wells) for contaminant transport to the ocean. The model simulations in this study also did not compare the effect of dry wells relative to the alternative of artificially directing runoff through surface storm drains. Natural surface flow routes may have soil and vegetation that can provide contaminant attenuation, but this attenuation may be substantially reduced in urban areas with lined or paved drainage systems (U.S. Environmental Protection Agency, 2001). Runoff routed through a dry well will also likely emerge at a different location (that may be more or less tolerant of contamination) than if it had been allowed to pass through the surface-water system. Whether dry wells increase or decrease, relative to natural or artificial surface-water drainage, the potential for contamination of receiving waters depends on conditions that are site specific and, therefore, beyond the scope of this study.

The results of the numerical simulations are reported to 0.1 percent of the concentration of the infiltration water. Greater precision may be needed in some cases, particularly where drinking-water standards are involved.

Advancing Understanding of the Effect of Dry Wells on Groundwater Quality

The study limitations discussed above are primarily imposed by the need for results that have island-wide applicability. If a more precise assessment is required, approaches and data that are more site specific are needed. For example, although many of the contaminants typical of road runoff worldwide are likely to be present in roadside dry wells in Hawai'i, concentrations may differ because of traffic, climate, and other factors. Other contaminants may also come from site-specific land uses near the dry wells. To more precisely assess the effects of dry wells on the Island of Hawai'i, the specific types and concentrations of contaminants entering the dry wells need to be identified because each contaminant reacts with the water and aquifer in different ways, which can affect their concentrations in groundwater. Approaches to determining the types and concentrations of contaminants entering dry wells include sampling and analysis of water and sediment. Automated monitoring systems can collect multiple water samples to show how concentrations vary over time. Analysis of sediment in the dry well offers another approach to studying the contaminants that enter a dry well over a long period, because many contaminants in road runoff adsorb onto suspended sediment particles. Water samples can also be collected from potential receiving waters and analyzed for contaminants detected in the water entering the dry well, although it may be difficult to definitively tie any contaminants detected to dry wells.

Determining flow paths on a site-specific basis can provide information on the connection between specific dry wells and receiving waters and could take into account the effect of local hydrogeologic features and multiple, closely spaced wells. Some subsurface hydrogeologic structures may be difficult to detect in monitor wells or other subsurface borings but may be detected using geophysical techniques. A more direct approach to determining groundwater flow paths for a specific area is to inject a tracer such as a dye into a dry well and monitor where it emerges. Positive results can help determine whether a direct groundwater flow path exists between a dry well and receiving waters and the time it will take the contaminant to travel this path.

Determining detrimental contaminant concentrations is key to connecting the effect of dry wells on water quality with the impact on the receiving water. Determining these concentrations is primarily an ecological or public-health issue, and concentration limits are normally established by the agencies tasked with protecting the receiving waters.

Data and analyses from these site-specific approaches can contribute incrementally toward a more complete understanding of the effect of dry wells on groundwater quality. Studies focused on a specific site, however, can be costly and have limited relevance to other areas. The results of this study can help determine which dry wells are likely to have the greatest effect on nearby receiving waters and where the greatest needs for site-specific studies are.

Summary and Conclusions

Widespread use of dry wells to dispose of urban runoff has raised concern about potential effects on quality of groundwater on the Island of Hawai'i. When water and contaminants infiltrate the ground through the dry well, they pass through the unsaturated zone of the aquifer then recharge the saturated aquifer. The contaminants form a plume in the saturated aquifer. Contaminant concentrations in the plume are attenuated by advection and hydrodynamic dispersion as they travel with the regional groundwater flow. The thickness of the unsaturated zone, the hydraulic properties of the aquifer, and the rate of regional groundwater flux affect the contaminant concentrations in the aquifer. The objective of this study was to assess the potential effects of dry wells for the entire Island of Hawai'i.

This study used semi-generic numerical models of groundwater flow and solute (contaminant) transport to assess the potential effect of dry wells on groundwater quality on the Island of Hawai'i. The semi-generic models are generalized numerical models that have a range of aquifer properties and regional groundwater gradients that are characteristic for the island as indicated in previous studies. Several semi-generic models were created to study the effect of dry wells in different conditions, such as different unsaturated-zone thicknesses or different aquifer characteristics from one location to the next. End members of the range were represented by conditions in the Kona and Hilo areas, both of which are situated on high-permeability lava flow aquifers but have contrasting climates and regional groundwater flow. In all simulations, dry-well infiltration and contamination were simulated with an infiltration pulse of 5 ft^3/s for 1 hour containing a hypothetical nonreactive contaminant.

Results of this study indicate that mixing of contaminated water from the surface with contaminant-free water in the saturated aquifer immediately reduces the contaminant concentration. How much the concentration is reduced depends on the rate at which the infiltration water and its contaminant are introduced as recharge to the saturated aquifer. This rate, in turn, depends on the hydraulic properties of the aquifer in a given area, the thickness of the unsaturated zone, and whether the infiltration is focused in a small area (such as in a dry well) or a large area (such as under natural conditions).

Model results indicate that infiltration of contaminated runoff through a dry well can substantially increase contaminant concentrations in the underlying saturated aquifer relative to infiltration under natural conditions. Simulated concentrations directly beneath a dry well were nearly eight times higher than the simulated concentrations directly beneath a broad infiltration area representing the natural condition. Infiltration through a dry well is concentrated in a small area compared to natural conditions, thus the infiltration pulse moves downward through the unsaturated zone more quickly and contaminants are delivered to the saturated aquifer in a shorter time. Focusing the infiltration over a small area also forces the contaminated infiltration water to mix initially with a smaller volume of uncontaminated water in the saturated aquifer.

Model results indicate that concentrations in the saturated aquifer are lower when the unsaturated zone beneath the dry well is thicker and higher when the unsaturated zone is thinner. A thicker unsaturated zone will result in an infiltration pulse that will be more drawn out in the unsaturated zone and cause contaminants to be delivered to the saturated aquifer more gradually.

Model results indicate that concentrations decline quickly as the contaminant plume migrates, with the regional groundwater flow, away from the dry well. The differences among concentrations resulting from the various unsaturated-zone thicknesses also diminish with distance from the dry well. At a horizontal distance of about 700 ft downgradient from dry wells, all simulated maximum concentrations were less than 1 percent of the concentration in the infiltration water; at about 0.5 mi downgradient from the dry well, all simulated concentrations were 0.1 percent or less. Actual concentrations may be lower than indicated by the models because of processes such as decay and reaction that were not simulated.

Differences from one location to the next also affect contaminant concentrations. The Hilo models differed from the Kona models in having a lower hydraulic conductivity but higher regional groundwater flux. The combination of more gradual recharge from the unsaturated zone stemming from the lower K_V and greater groundwater flux in the saturated zone result in lower overall concentrations in the Hilo models relative to comparable Kona models.

Model results are most sensitive to uncertainties in K_V, dispersivity, and porosity and specific yield. Results are less sensitive to uncertainties in K_H and the head gradient. The uncertainties primarily affect the area within a few hundred feet of the dry well. Model results were not sensitive to uncertainties in specific storage.

Results from the models can be used to assess how contaminants entering a dry well may affect receiving waters in a variety of situations on the Island of Hawai'i. The generalization that was necessary to make the results applicable island-wide, however, also limits the precision of the assessment. Better assessment would be obtained by using results from the semi-generic models having the most similar conditions (such as climate, hydraulic properties, regional groundwater gradient) to the dry well in question.

Limitations of this study imposed by the need for island-wide applicability can be overcome with more site-specific data and analyses. Studies focused on a specific site, however, can be costly and have limited relevance to other areas. The results of this study can help to determine which dry wells are likely to have the greatest effect on nearby receiving waters and where site-specific studies are most needed.

References Cited

Breault, R.F., and Granato, G.E., 2000, A synopsis of technical issues of concern for monitoring trace elements in highway and urban runoff: U.S. Geological Survey Open-File Report 00–422, 67 p.

Clague, D.A., and Dalrymple, G.B., 1987, The Hawaiian-Emperor volcanic chain, *in* Decker, R.W., Wright, T.L., and Stauffer, P.H., eds., Volcanism in Hawaii: U.S. Geological Survey Professional Paper 1350, v. 1, p. 5–54.

De Carlo, E.H., and Anthony, S.S., 2002, Spatial and temporal variability of trace element concentrations in an urban subtropical watershed, Honolulu, Hawaii: Applied Geochemistry, v. 17, p. 475–492.

De Carlo, E.H., Beltran, V.L., and Tomlinson, M.S., 2004, Composition of water and suspended sediment in streams of urbanized subtropical watersheds in Hawaii: Applied Geochemistry, v. 19, p. 1011–1037.

Departments of Public Works of the State of Hawaii, 1984, Standard details for public works construction: Departments of Public Works of the State of Hawaii, 207 p.

Giambelluca, T.W, Nullet, M.A., and Schroeder, T.A., 1986, Rainfall atlas of Hawaii: Honolulu, State of Hawaii Department of Land and Natural Resources, Division of Water and Land, Development Report no. R76, 267 p.

Gingerich, S.B., 2008, Ground-water availability in the Wailuku area, Maui, Hawai'i: U.S. Geological Survey Scientific Investigations Report 2008–5236, 95 p.

Gingerich, S.B., and Voss, C.I., 2005, Three-dimensional variable-density flow simulation of a coastal aquifer in southern Oahu, Hawaii, USA: Hydrogeology Journal, v. 13, p. 436–450.

Göbel, P. Dierkes, C., and Coldewey, W.G., 2007, Storm water runoff concentration matrix for urban areas: Journal of Contaminant Hydrology, v. 91, p. 26–42.

Grant, S.B., Rekhi, N.V., Pise, N.R., Reeves, R.L., Matsumoto, M., Wistrom, A., Moussa, L., Bay, S., and Kayhanian, M., 2003, A review of the contaminants and toxicity associated with particles in stormwater runoff: Caltrans CTSW-RT-03-059.73.15, 72 p. [http://www.dot.ca.gov/hq/env/ stormwater/pdf/CTSW-RT-03-059.pdf, accessed June 4, 2009].

Harbaugh, A.W., 2005, MODFLOW-2005, The U.S. Geological Survey modular ground-water model; the ground-water flow process: U.S. Geological Survey Techniques and Methods 6–A16, variously p.

Harbaugh, A.W., Banta, E.R., Hill, M.C., and McDonald, M.G., 2000, MODFLOW–2000, the U.S. Geological Survey modular ground-water model; user guide to modularization concepts and the ground-water flow process: U.S. Geological Survey Open-File Report 00–92, 121 p.

Hawai'i State Department of Business, Economic Development and Tourism, 2008, Hawaii State GIS Program; judicial boundaries: [http://hawaii.gov/dbedt/gis/judicial.htm, accessed April 24, 2009].

Hawai'i State Land Use Commission, 2002, Findings of fact, conclusions of law, and decision and order for a state land use district boundary amendment Docket A00–732: [http://luc.state.hi.us/cohawaii/a00-732tsa.pdf, accessed September 15, 2009].

Hunt, C.D, 1996, Geohydrology of the Island of Oahu, Hawaii: U.S. Geological Survey Professional Paper 1412–B, 54 p.

Hunt, C.D., Jr., 2007, Ground-water nutrient flux to coastal waters and numerical simulation of wastewater injection at Kihei, Maui, Hawaii: U.S. Geological Survey Scientific Investigations Report 2006–5283, 69 p.

Izuka, S.K., Senter, C.A., and Johnson, A.G., 2009, Reconnaissance assessment of the potential for roadside dry wells to affect water quality on the Island of Hawai'i: U.S. Geological Survey Scientific Investigations Report 2009–5249, 55 p.

Langevin, C.D., Thorne, D.T., Jr., Dausman, A.M., Sukop, M.C., and Guo, Weixing, 2008, SEAWAT Version 4; a computer program for simulation of multi-species solute and heat transport: U.S. Geological Survey Techniques and Methods Book 6, Chapter A22, 39 p.

Macdonald, G.A., Abbott, A.T., and Peterson, F.L., 1983, Volcanoes in the sea, the geology of Hawaii: Honolulu, University of Hawaii Press, 517 p.

McDonald, M.G., and Harbaugh, A.W., 1988, A modular three-dimensional finite difference ground-water flow model: U.S. Geological Survey Techniques of Water-Resources Investigations, Book 6, Chapter A1, 586 p.

Mikkelsen, P.S., Häflinger, M., Ochs, M., Tjell, J.C., Jacobsen, P., and Boller, M., 1996, Experimental assessment of soil and groundwater contamination from two old infiltration systems for road run-off in Switzerland: The Science of the Total Environment, v. 189/190, p. 341–347.

National Climatic Data Center, 2010, Hilo International Airport Hilo, HI, United States: [http://www4.ncdc.noaa.gov/cgi-win/wwcgi.dll?wwDI~StnSrch~StnID~20023247, accessed November 23, 2010].

National Weather Service, 2009, Hydrometeorological design studies center precipitation frequency data server: [http://hdsc.nws.noaa.gov/hdsc/pfds/pfds_maps.html, accessed January 25, 2011].

Niswonger, R.G., Prudic, D.E., and Regan, R.S., 2006, Documentation of the Unsaturated-Zone Flow (UZF1) Package for modeling unsaturated flow between the land surface and the water table with MODFLOW-2005: U.S. Geological Survey Techniques and Methods 6–A19, 62 p.

Oki, D.S.,1999, Geohydrology and numerical simulation of the ground-water flow system of Kona, Island of Hawaii: U.S. Geological Survey Water-Resources Investigations Report 99–4070, 49 p.

Oki, D.S., 2002, Reassessment of ground-water recharge and simulated ground-water availability for the Hawi area of North Kohala, Hawaii: U.S. Geological Survey Water-Resources Investigations Report 02–4006, 62 p.

Oki, D.S., 2005, Numerical simulation of the effects of low-permeability valley-fill barriers and the redistribution of ground-water withdrawals in the Pearl Harbor area, Oahu, Hawaii: U.S. Geological Survey Scientific Investigations Report 2005–5253, 111 p.

Oki, D.S., Tribble, G.W., Souza, W.R., and Bolke, E.L., 1999, Ground-water resources in Kaloko Honokohau National Historical Park, Island of Hawaii, and numerical simulation of the effects of groundwater withdrawals: U.S. Geological Survey Water-Resources Investigations Report 99–4070, 49 p.

Peterson, D.W., and Moore, R.B., 1987, Geologic History and Evolution of geologic concepts, Island of Hawaii, in Decker, R.W., Wright, T.L., and Stauffer, P.H., eds., Volcanism in Hawaii: U.S. Geological Survey Professional Paper 1350, v. 1, p. 149–198.

Presley, T.K., Jamison, M.T.J., and Young, S.T.M., 2008, Rainfall, discharge, and water-quality data during stormwater monitoring, July 1, 2007, to June 30, 2008; Halawa Stream drainage basin and the H-1 storm drain, Oahu, Hawaii: U.S. Geological Survey Open-File Report 2008–1233, 46 p.

Sato, H.T., Ikeda, W., Paeth, R., Smythe, R., and Yakehiro, M., 1973, Soil survey of the island of Hawaii, State of Hawaii: U.S. Department of Agriculture, Soil Conservation Service, 115 p. plus maps.

Sherrod, D.R., Sinton, J.M., Watkins, S.E., and Brunt, K.M., 2008, Geologic map of the State of Hawai'i: U.S. Geological Survey Open–File Report 2007–1089, 83 p., 8 plates, scales 1:100,000 and 1:250,000, with GIS database.

Souza, W.R., and Voss, C.I., 1987, Analysis of an anisotropic coastal aquifer system using variable-density flow and solute transport simulation: Journal of Hydrology, v. 92, p. 17–41.

Stearns, H.T., and Macdonald, G.A., 1946, Geology and ground-water resources of the island of Hawaii: Hawaii Division of Hydrography, Bulletin 9, 303 p., 1 plate.

Thomas, D.M., Paillet, F.L., and Conrad, M.E., 1996, Hydrogeology of the Hawaii Scientific Drilling Project borehole KP–1, 2; groundwater geochemistry and regional flow patterns: Journal of Geophysical Research, v. 101, p. 11,683–11,694.

Underwood, M.R., Meyer, W., and Souza, W.R., 1995, Ground-water availability from the Hawi Aquifer in the Kohala area, Hawaii: U.S. Geological Survey Water-Resources Investigations Report 95–4113, 57 p.

U.S. Environmental Protection Agency, 1994, Potential groundwater contamination from intentional and nonintentional stormwater infiltration: EPA/600/SR-94/051, 7 p.

U.S. Environmental Protection Agency, 1999, The Class V Underground Injection Control study, volume 3, storm water drainage wells: EPA/816-R-99-014c, 96 p.

U.S. Environmental Protection Agency, 2001, Managing storm water runoff to prevent contamination of drinking water: Source Water Protection Bulletin, EPA 816-F-01-020, 7 p.

U.S. Environmental Protection Agency, 2007, Class V injection wells: [http://www.epa.gov/OGWDW/uic/class5/index.html, accessed November 14, 2008].

U.S. Geological Survey, 2010, National Water Information System; web interface, groundwater levels for Hawaii: [http://nwis.waterdata.usgs.gov/hi/nwis/gwlevels, accessed November 23, 2010].

Western Region Climate Center, 2010, Station daily summary, Kaloko-Honokohau, Hawaii: [http://www.wrcc.dri.edu/cgi-bin/rawMAIN.pl?hiHKAL, accessed December 14, 2010].

Whittier, R.B., Rotzoll, K., Dhal, S., El-Kadi, A.I., Ray, C., Chen, G., and Chang, D., 2004, Island of Hawaii Source Water Assessment Program report: Honolulu, University of Hawaii, Water Resources Research Center, Hawaii Source Water Assessment Program report, v. II, 65 p.

Wolff, R.H., and Wong, M.F., 2008, Effects of the H-3 highway stormwater runoff on the water quality of Halawa Stream, Oahu, Hawaii, November 1998 to August 2004: U.S. Geological Survey Scientific Investigations Report 2008–5034, 78 p.

Zheng, Chunmiao, and Wang, P.W., 1999, MT3DMS; a modular three-dimensional multispecies transport model for simulation of advection, dispersion, and chemical reactions of contaminants in groundwater systems; documentation and user's guide: U.S. Army Corps of Engineers Engineer Research and Development Center Contract Report SERDP–99–1, 221 p.

Produced in the Western Region, Menlo Park, California
Manuscript approved for publication, May 12, 2011
Edited by J.L. Zigler
Layout by David R. Jones

Izuka—Potential Effects of Roadside Dry Wells on Groundwater Quality on the Island of Hawai'i—SIR 2011–5072